Jewish Voice for Peace is a n
that supports the aspirations ~~of Israelis and Palestinians for~~
security and self-determination.

We seek:

- A U.S. foreign policy based on promoting peace, democracy, human rights, and respect for international law
- An end to the Israeli occupation of the West Bank, the Gaza Strip, and East Jerusalem
- A resolution of the Palestinian refugee problem consistent with international law and equity
- An end to all violence against civilians
- Peace among the peoples of the Middle East

ISBN:9760806-0-5

©2004, Jewish Voice for Peace

For more copies, contact us at info@jewishvoiceforpeace.org or 510-465-1777.

Editors: Henri Picciotto and Mitchell Plitnick
Book design: Norma Mark
Cover design: Roni Terkel, Cecilie Surasky

www.JewishVoiceforPeace.org

CONTENTS

Introduction
Mitchell Plitnick and Henri Picciotto ii

1 Reclaiming the Struggle Against Anti-Semitism
Mitchell Plitnick 1

2 In Search of Anti-Semitism at the World Social Forum
Cecilie Surasky 13

3 No, It's Not Anti-Semitic
Judith Butler 21

4 What is "Anti-Semitism" and Does It Still Exist?
Terry Fletcher 37

5 Bogus Charges
Henri Picciotto 45

6 Discrimination, Racism and Anti-Semitism in our Community
Laurie Polster 51

7 Historical US Anti-Semitism— The Invisible Oppression: Stereotyping, Scapegoating, Discounting
Penny Rosenwasser 59

8 Is Criticizing Israel Anti-Semitic?
Chuck Sher 85

INTRODUCTION

Jewish Voice for Peace is a national grassroots organization that supports the aspirations of Israelis and Palestinians for security and self-determination. In its many dimensions, anti-Semitism is always a part of our awareness. Like Jews everywhere, we carry the burden of the history of anti-Semitism. It is often that very history that inspires Jewish work for social justice, and this is indeed the case for many of us.

If our involvement in Middle East peace work has taught us anything, it is that fear and complexity can paralyze even the most dynamic of individuals and organizations. One of the fears we face is that our challenges to the policies of the Israeli government will be interpreted as anti-Semitic. One of the complexities is that some have equated all criticism of Israel with anti-Semitism, while some anti-Semites have used the Palestinian cause to mask their hatred of Jews. Nevertheless, we refuse to get stuck: drawing our inspiration from Jewish tradition, we work for peace, social justice, and human rights, even if our stance is unpopular in some circles, and even if we need to do a lot of talking and writing to clarify our thoughts.

This booklet is part of this process. Most of the articles are by members of JVP. They reflect our diversity, and will help us deepen our collective understanding of this crucial topic.

We are also honored to reprint Berkeley scholar Judith Butler's London Review of Books piece on this subject.

We hope that you find these articles useful, and that you will be encouraged to join us in the fight against all forms of bigotry. As one of our members, a Holocaust survivor, puts it: "Never again–for anyone!"

Henri Picciotto
Mitchell Plitnick
Jewish Voice for Peace

ARTICLE 1

RECLAIMING THE STRUGGLE AGAINST ANTI-SEMITISM

Mitchell Plitnick

Those of us who are involved in activism around Israel/Palestine and take a position critical of the standard American and Israeli views of the conflict are constantly peppered with accusations of anti-Semitism; or, in the case of Jews, we are told we are "self-hating." Indeed, for Jews active on this issue, it becomes incumbent upon us to prominently and frequently argue that criticism of Israel is not anti-Semitic.

It can get frustrating. Constantly engaging in the same argument is bad enough, but when that argument is over something that should be obvious—such as the right to criticize the actions of a state with one of the world's strongest militaries, that has been in occupation of another people for 37 years—the argument becomes all the more tiresome. In fact, it can become so tiresome that many people—both Jewish and non-Jewish—who have to deal with it can easily become so frustrated that they cannot or do not wish to hear about genuine issues of anti-Semitism. It is becoming the cry of "wolf" that can portend a horrible fate down the road.

The argument has frequently been very disruptive to opposition to American policies in the Middle East. This was demonstrated in March of 2003 in the very unfortunate flap over Michael Lerner's absence from the invited speakers' list at a major anti-war demonstration in San Francisco. Indeed, charges of anti-Semitism, both merited and not, have been dogging anti-war movements in the United States for years.

What is it we speak of when talking about anti-Semitism? The term itself is a source of some controversy. The term "Semite" refers to a linguistic group which includes both Arabic and Hebrew (most other Semitic languages have fallen into disuse). The term "anti-Semitism" was coined by a German Jew-hater, Wilhelm Marr, in the late 19th century. He coined the phrase to refer to a new form of Judeophobia, one which is based on purported racial characteristics. In order to have a term that was easier to pass along than "Judenhass" (hatred of Jews), and to have a new phrase for his theory — one which denied the European heritage of European Jewry — he took what was at the time an obscure linguistic term and applied it to his racial theory of Jews. Ironically, anti-Semitism was coined against Jews alone, despite the fact that at the time exceedingly few Jews spoke Hebrew. Even to this day, it has been many centuries since any Semitic language was the primary language of the majority of Jews worldwide. Arabs, on the other hand, are, by definition, Semites, but were beyond the racist consciousness of Marr, who never encountered them.

The Holocaust was the ultimate expression of Marr's racial conception of anti-Semitism; all the more so because it was different in character and nature from the centuries of persecution on religious grounds that Jews had faced in Europe. The effects were devastating and reach beyond the unimaginable death and torment the Nazi persecution caused (not only to Jews. It helps to recall that millions of others were slaughtered in the camps as well, though we were the primary targets). The trauma of the Holocaust for all Jews, especially Europeans, remains very much with us to this day. The Holocaust represented the ultimate betrayal of Jewish hopes that the modern, secular ideologies of socialism, communism and liberalism would at last free us from centuries of persecution. It convinced many Jews that we would always be at risk; that at any moment, no matter how good things seemed, the pogroms and exile would start all over again, and that the world does, and would always, hate us. Entire Jewish movements virtually died in the Holocaust (including non-Zionist nationalist movements).

But there were other effects as well, contrary to what one might expect. Institutionalized discrimination against Jews in the West came under fierce attack as shame over what had been done in Europe spread. It was not an immediate process, of course; the practice of barring Jews from entry into various neighborhoods or clubs persisted in the United States into the 1970s. Nevertheless today, with few exceptions, most Jews live freely without any significant social obstacles to employment or finding homes.

This needs to be cause for Jewish celebration. We must not forget the Holocaust, nor ignore the fact that some of our greatest historical tragedies have come on the heels of some of our greatest periods of prosperity. But the road to sustaining our security lies not in fear of a repeat of our greatest trauma, but in vigilance, consciousness and cooperation with our many allies in creating a world where all forms of hatred based on religion, ethnicity, gender, sexual orientation or any other innate characteristics have no power to threaten people.

Does this mean that anti-Semitism no longer exists? Indeed not. In the United States, many white supremacist groups (the KKK, neo-Nazi groups, Christian Identity groups and others) continue their campaigns against Jews as well as women, GLBT folks and, of course, people of color. More and more, the relative success of Jews in the United States and some parts of Europe has spawned some reactionary rekindling of late 19th/early 20th century Jewish conspiracy theories, harkening back to the infamous Russian forgery, The Protocols of the Elders of Zion (a Czarist era tract purporting to dictate a Jewish/Masonic program of global domination). Still, it must be understood that, as potentially dangerous and certainly disturbing as these things are, they do not represent anything like the sorts of obstacles and threats in day-to-day living that many disenfranchised and oppressed people face all the time, and which have been all too familiar throughout much of our history. Again, this should be a cause for celebration among Jews.

More recently, a great deal of attention has been focused on anti-Semitism in the anti-war movement. This can be a difficult tangle. Supporters of Israel have worked hard to nearly erase the distinction between legitimate criticism of Israel and the occupation and anti-Semitism. However, it is a simple fact that there is a segment of the left that believes in Jewish conspiracy theories. We hear it at many events criticizing Israel, the war on Iraq and the dual occupations in the Persian Gulf and the West Bank and Gaza. Last year, we heard it from a member of Congress, James Moran, who said that the United States would not be going to war with Iraq were it not for "the Jews".

No one would dispute the fact that AIPAC (the American-Israel Public Affairs Committee) wields a great deal of influence on Capitol Hill. However, American foreign policy in the Middle East has remained remarkably consistent since the end of the 1967 war, which was well before AIPAC had grown its power. Israel's position as a steadfast ally of the United States has been a centerpiece of American foreign policy formation since that time. However, as more attention has been paid to the Middle East since September 11, 2001, the idea that "the Jews" are pulling the strings on American policy has gained more currency. Far easier than trying to take on the behemoth that is the American government, the Christian Right, and the arms industry, as well as decades of entrenched policy, this view targets the relatively small group that has served as the mouthpiece for so many other forces. The forces that motivate the ill-advised and often immoral American policy in Israel/Palestine are complicated. A Jewish conspiracy is much simpler.

This view is not only harmful to the anti-war movement, but more importantly, it is morally repugnant. While remaining the view of only a small minority of the anti-war movement, it is a vocal minority view, and one that the majority of the anti-war movement is doing little to silence.

Our role as Jewish activists working for a just peace in Israel/Palestine and against the American war in Iraq is to provide the leadership needed for the left to stand against this kind of hate. Supporters of Israel, whether intentionally or not, have contributed to this rise of anti-Semitism with their bullying tactics in Congress and the media . They have worked to enhance the perception of the political strength of Jewish groups while obscuring the role of American global designs, the arms industry and, especially, the Christian Right in creating the political pressure in support of Israel in Washington. They are then turning around and bemoaning the "rise of anti-Semitism on the left". It is thus the responsibility of progressive Jews to both challenge the Jewish conspiracy theories of some on the left, and oppose the groups like AIPAC that foment them.

When we consider these questions, we must bear in mind that while anti-Semitism, in its myriad forms, has ebbed and flowed over the centuries, few indeed are the periods in our history that match the level of security and prosperity Jews have found in the United States and Western Europe today. Yet, make mention of this, and many of us become defensive, as if the thought that things are so good for Jews, relative to our history, threatens to put us off our guard, so that if danger rises again we would not be prepared to meet it and survive. It is crucial for the long-term health of the Jewish people that we strike a much better balance between recognizing how good things are for Jews where most of us are living today, and with being vigilant against the return of darker times.

When it comes to the issues around Israel, the question of anti-Semitism takes on much greater importance. Much is made of growing anti-Semitism in the Arab world. In Arab countries there are exceedingly few Jews, in most none at all, and all the Jews most people in those countries see are Israeli leaders, soldiers and settlers, and occasional American Jews who voice views at least as hawkish. This has made Arab countries fertile lands for growing anti-Jewish conspiracy theories and for sparking ideas about Jews that were once far more prevalent in Christendom than in the Muslim world.

Still, it is easy to see why people would see such a phenomenon as proof that the Arab, and particularly the Palestinian view of the conflict with Israel is motivated not by dispossession or concern over Western domination of the Middle East, but by the hatred of Jews. When a group of people are absent from one's life, and one sees only frightening images of them, this creates the best atmosphere for bigotry to flourish. There is little reason for Arabs to distinguish between the actions of the Israeli government, of which they see only the very worst, and the Jewish people, who are purportedly represented by the Jewish State.

Thus, the proliferation of sales of *The Protocols of the Elders of Zion* and the occasional quotes from some Arab and Muslim leaders that reflect great hostility to Jews are eagerly picked up by the mainstream media. We see a classic example of this in the recent, repulsive attack on Jews by the Malaysian Prime Minister, Mahathir Muhammed. In a speech otherwise devoted to admonishing the Muslim world to do a better job of bringing itself into the modern world, Mahathir stated that "the Jews run the world by proxy," feeding into populist anti-Jewish sentiments.

Of course, there were those in the Arab world who had antipathy for Jews well before the state of Israel and even the Zionist movement were established (in particular, the Palestinian struggle remains scarred by its leader in the 30s and 40s, Hajj Amin al-Husayni, whose anti-Jewish remarks and actions simply cannot be written off as a Palestinian reaction to the growth of the Zionist movement and the settlement of Palestine), but it is a historical reality that, although Jews did not generally enjoy legal rights equal to Muslims in most of the Arab and Muslim world, our experience there was far better, far more free from persecution, than our experience in Europe. It might not have been a paradise of equality, and to be sure, there were some very outrageous acts against Jews from time to time, but in the context of the times the Jewish experience in the Muslim world was far better than the experience of Jews and other minorities elsewhere.

The question in the U.S. is made even more complicated by the presence of real anti-Semites on both sides. Dispensationalist Christian evangelicals, such as Jerry Falwell and Pat Robertson, promote their end-of-days vision—which depends on a fulfillment of the prophecy of a Jewish return to Zion—where Armageddon will see the Jews all converted or destroyed, with a fanatical support of Israel. It is worthwhile to remember that this branch of right-wing Christianity is the source of much of the power of the incorrectly-named "Jewish lobby." The Christian Right is what gives pro-Israel lobbying its voter power, generates stacks of letters to representatives, and pressures editorial boards with potential loss of circulation. There just aren't enough Jews on the planet to have that kind of impact, and, anti-Jewish rhetoric notwithstanding, the greatest concentration of power continues to rest in the same hands it has for centuries.

Right-wing Christian support for Israel, motivated not by love of Jews but antipathy for us, is a threat that must be confronted, yet the major Jewish organizations have steadfastly refused to do this because of their support of Israel.

One need only recall, when the Monica Lewinsky scandal was in high gear and Bill Clinton exerted some pressure on Netanyahu to compromise with the Palestinians (eventually leading to the Wye Accords, hardly a major compromise for Israel), Netanyahu responded by coming to America and visiting his "good friend" Falwell before greeting the U.S. President. Mere weeks later, Falwell gave a speech in which he stated that the anti-Christ would be a Jew. It is thus rather difficult to see Falwell as a man with the best interests of the Jewish people at heart. This is only one small example of a much greater problem.

Some White supremacists such as David Duke have adopted a pro-Palestinian façade in order to promote their hatred of Jews. Although these characters have remained on the periphery of the movement for Palestinian rights, some of their thinking has gained more and more momentum within the movement. This is reflected in an alarming increase in the belief that Israel controls the U.S. with regard to the Middle East. This assertion falls apart in the face of the facts (among many good works on this point, Stephen Zunes' recent book, "Tinderbox" is one of the best, as is much of the work on this subject by Noam Chomsky.) This does harken back to the sorts of Jewish conspiracy theories discussed earlier, although in many cases, people who believe this theory may be acting out of a lack of facts rather than antipathy for Jews. There is no doubt that the lobby that supports Israel is very powerful in Congress, and the media activism of Israel's supporters has been remarkably effective. It is also true that, while the Christian Right may provide a lot of the financial and people-power of this activism, the Jewish groups are providing the public face and most of the leadership. It is crucial that we keep in mind that it is not always easy to know the motivations of others. Thus, it is imperative that we attack ideas of a worldwide Jewish conspiracy as anti-Semitic while being very judicious about confusing those who are misled but are truly working for what they see as justice with those who truly wish to harm Jews simply because we are Jews. All too often we fail to make this distinction and, as a result, fail to win friends where we can and alienating potential allies instead.

For many, Jews and non-Jews alike, all of this means seeing anti-Semitism everywhere. For some, it creates the perfect climate to shield Israel from all criticism by equating all such criticism with anti-Semitism. The process is not always so simple. Many allow certain criticisms, but draw a line beyond which lies only anti-Semitism. It is not always easy, or even possible, to know what motivates the opinions of others. But whatever one's views on the question of Israel and Palestine, elemental reason dictates that opposition to Israel's policies, including the occupation, the rejection of all claims against it by the Palestinian refugees of 1948 and the laws that give Jews rights above non-Jews, can be and often is based on rationales that include no antipathy whatsoever towards Jews. This is not to say that such arguments cannot be made out of anti-Semitism, only that the arguments can be made for many other reasons as well.

The debate and discussion is a fair one to have. The situation in Palestine/Israel, while it has many elements in common with other conflicts, is also different from most in that the powerful group can easily see itself as the victim, as Jews have been for so much of our history. Progress toward reconciliation has been consistently stalled by rhetoric and name-calling. As Jews working for a future where Palestinians and Israeli Jews live together in mutual respect, peace and security, as well against the effects of institutionalized bigotry of all kinds, it is high time that we took the fight against anti-Semitism from those who use it both to legitimize policies and actions that oppress others and to stifle legitimate debate over issues that touch millions of lives.

We do this by confronting anti-Semitism where it really exists, whatever the source, and by confronting with equal vigor those, whether Jewish or not, who dishonor the millions of victims and centuries of persecution of Jews. By cynically manipulating charges of anti-Semitism for their own ends, they defend policies that are antithetical to the justice and universal equality that is necessary for Jews and all other historical victims of oppression to live in peace and security.

Mitchell Plitnick is the Director of Education and Policy for Jewish Voice for Peace. Raised Orthodox, Plitnick spent over 20 years studying Jewish and Israeli history. His articles have appeared in publications across the US and around the world.

ARTICLE 2

IN SEARCH OF ANTI-SEMITISM AT THE WORLD SOCIAL FORUM

Cecilie Surasky

It is my first morning at the World Social Forum in Mumbai, India and I am at a workshop on Palestinian women and the occupation. In the audience is a woman who I first think might be Israeli—she could easily be one of my friends and I feel an immediate kinship with her. She tells me she is 34 and has lived her whole life in Gaza except for college. I ask her if I can interview her.

She cautiously eyes my card, on which I have purposely written in thick, visible letters: Jewish Voice for Peace. "I don't know," she says. "Do you support the occupation?" It seems such a surreal question. How could anyone support an occupation? The very word evokes domination, a kind of cruelty. No, I say, we want to end the occupation. We want a peace that is just.

I ask about the checkpoints. She describes sitting in her car waiting to be allowed to drive through. The young Israeli soldiers are in sniper posts. You can't see them, but they can see you, she explains. They signal it's time to go by shooting their guns. She waits a long time until the soldiers say, "OK, now the dogs can go."

"You think, 'Do I want to be called a dog, or do I just want to go?'" she tells me. "I don't care, so I start my car and they yell 'No! Not you, I said dogs!'" So she turns her car off, and sometime later they say, "OK, now humans can go!" She starts her car and they look at her and the others and say "No! I said humans." And she turns her car off and waits until finally this "other" category of Palestinian—neither human nor animal—is allowed to pass.

"This," she says, "is my only contact with Israelis." And this, I think, and is my first contact with someone from Gaza.

The WSF and the new anti-Semitism

The World Social Forum (WSF) is the populist answer to the World Economic Forum in Davos, Switzerland. Instead of a gathering of the world's mostly wealthy, white, and male heads of state and captains of industry in Davos, the WSF is a cacophony of anti-globalization/human rights activists from all over the globe.

The roughly 100,000 participants represent every imaginable cause—from Indian "untouchables" and Bhutanese refugees to child trafficking and sexual minorities. They are seen in the hundreds of marches that seem to appear out of nowhere down the main thoroughfare, at the 500 information booths, in more than 1,000 workshops, and on the political posters filling every inch of available wall space.

I have come, like most attendees, to connect with others working on international human rights. But I have an additional reason for being here. The Simon Wiesenthal Center (SWC) has cited the WSF as one of the centers of what it and others refer to as the "new anti-Semitism", and these charges have been picked up by various journalists as evidence of a dangerous new trend on the left.

Upon closer reading, most of these accounts make little if any distinction at all between anti-Semitism and criticism of Israel, or between anti-Semitism and anti-Zionism. The SWC description of the "anti-Jewish" atmosphere at last year's WSF in Brazil is one of these accounts.

And yet, their description of the WSF is so disturbing, even frightening, that I am prepared to encounter at minimum silent hostility, and possibly even physical attacks from my fellow attendees. I have come to the WSF to be loudly and visibly Jewish, to make a presentation that deconstructs the theory that Jews dictate U.S. policy in the Middle East, and to see for myself this purported new tidal wave of hatred of Jews from the rest of the global left.

The conference is not what I expected

It is surprising to find that the Israel-Palestine conflict and the occupation are not more prominently featured at the conference. Out of hundreds of ongoing marches, I witness only one small pro-Palestine march, which includes a prominent Israeli leftist marching in the front row.

Out of about 500 information stalls, only two represent Palestinian human rights groups: PENGON, which is working to tear down the wall Israel is building through Palestinian land, and Al-Haq, which is launching a campaign identifying collective punishment as a war crime. Of the thousands of political posters, I see only one series—Al-Haq's powerful posters on collective punishment—related to the issue.

I attend most of the workshops I can find on the Israel-Palestine issue. What I do not hear (or see) is anything I would consider anti-Semitic. In a global conference of 100,000 people, one expects to hear an enormous range of political perspectives, including the occasional extreme or intolerant remark. Given that I am prepared for the worst, I am shocked that the overwhelming majority of what is said in workshops critical of U.S. and Israeli policies in the territories is milder than the articles and essays one can read in Israeli newspapers on any given day.

Two realities, one anti-Semitism industry

After I return home, the Wiesenthal Center publishes an alarming piece entitled "Networking to Destroy Israel" in the *Jerusalem Post*. The article claims that this year's WSF was "hijacked by anti-American and anti-Israeli forces" and leads me to wonder whether we attended the same conference. In this piece, and for the second year in a row, they strangely declare themselves the only Jewish NGO to attend the WSF. (I personally saw participants from Brit Tzedek and Yesh Gvul, to name just a few—and Jewish Voice for Peace is listed in the official program.)

They go on to cite a litany of statements, including mine, as proof that the WSF is a place where people who want to destroy Israel meet to plot and recruit. Employing a form of twisted logic that would make Donald Rumsfeld proud, they essentially claim that the absence of any blatant anti-Semitism is not proof that there was none, but merely an indication of a more "sophisticated" kind of anti-Zionism (and therefore anti-Semitism) in which sympathetic Jews such as Jewish Voice for Peace (JVP) play a starring roll.

The account is so riddled with errors—I am misquoted,

JVP is described as "campus-based", all of my colleagues are given the wrong attributions, and quoted either inaccurately or out of context—that it is pointless to list them all. (In their full report available on their website, they inexplicably claim that I called on groups to boycott Starbucks. I heard no one make this call at the entire conference, and even so, the call as they report it actually violates JVP's guidelines.)

The op-ed contains bits of truth but strings together isolated statements to make them sound like a tidal wave of hatred and part of what they call an "orchestrated" and "insidious" campaign to destroy Israel.

All this begs the question of why a group such as the SWC would want to fuel hysteria about anti-Semitism in general, especially in regard to the left. The SWC has an important history of hunting down former Nazis, exposing the activities of neo-fascists and other right wing hate groups, and fighting genuine anti-Semitism.

But the SWC is like many other mainstream Jewish organizations in the United States that have expanded their mission from fighting the oppression of Jews by others to attempting to silence critics—including other Jews—of Israel's human rights record. These organizations' new role as arbiters of acceptable opinion is a far cry from their proud past. And it is ironic, given the spirited debate about Israel's occupation that takes place in Israel, but apparently is unacceptable in the rest of the world.

For many of these organizations, as evidenced in the SWC op-ed, the mere mention of the heartbreaking reality of Israel's occupation of the Palestinians is proof of an insidious plan supported by other Jews to wipe Israel off the face of the earth. Further, it is evidence of bias simply to point out causality–that groups like JVP or Al-Haq exist not because we are anti-Jewish or anti-Israel–but to end the injustices of Israel's occupation and treatment of Arabs, and to stop the spiral of revenge that has become a horrible tragedy for everyone.

To even the most casual observer, this is shocking for a community with a long tradition of protecting free speech, and an even longer tradition of embracing debate. It is also self-defeating given the now increasingly mainstream view both in Israel and the US that the occupation and militarization of Israeli culture is bad not just for Palestinians, but also for Israelis.

What is perhaps most troublesome is that by fueling the fires of fear through hyperbolic statements, (an easy thing to do to a people with our history of suffering and persecution) these groups—who say they represent all Jews— play a critical role in giving the current Israeli government permission to violate virtually every moral and ethical standard central to the Jewish tradition in its effort to keep down the Palestinians.

They make peace ever more distant by perpetuating the myth that Jews and Arabs, Israelis and Palestinians, have nothing to say to each other and are incapable of recognizing each other as full human beings with similar wants and needs. They get under our skin and seek to make Jews believe that indeed, the world is out to get us and we can trust no one.

Acts of loving kindness at the WSF: the untold story

In my own experience as a very "out" Jew at the conference, I felt no hate. Instead, I met a number of Palestinians and Arabs who, on some fundamental level, expressed the pain of separation. "I am Muslim, and we were raised to respect the Jewish tradition," a Palestinian woman living in Jordan told me. "We used to live next door to Jews, and we were friends."

After I spoke at a session about suspending military aid to Israel until it ends its occupation, and identified myself as a member of Jewish Voice for Peace, a Palestinian woman thanked me and a distinguished Lebanese man from Jordan came up and gave me a huge hug and a kiss.

Two of the Arabs that the SWC op-ed quoted most prominently in their description of what they called a campaign to destroy Israel were environmental scientist Rania Masri and activist journalist Ahmed Shawki.

Thirty minutes after meeting me for the first time at the Forum, Ahmed Shawki offered to loan me the new digital camera given to him by his wife. He knew I was eager to take pictures and the airline had misplaced my luggage. Knowing nothing of my politics, only that I was from a Jewish peace group, he gave me his digital camera.

The next day, the bag containing my passport, credit cards, and his camera was stolen. Our mutual friend and colleague from Lebanon, Rania Masri, handed me a hundred dollars from her wallet and absolutely insisted I take her ATM card and PIN number so I would have money for the rest of the trip. And Ahmed? To this day, Ahmed refuses to accept payment for the camera that was stolen.

This is the real story of Jews, Arabs, and the World Social Forum that needs to be told; that is, the ways in which we so quickly and easily recognize each other's fundamental humanity. As one young Arab-Israeli woman—who will never be quoted in an article about the rising tide of anti-Semitism—said so eloquently and passionately the last night of the conference, "Yes, I experience discrimination in Israel. But my friendship with Jewish Israelis is proof that it is a lie when both sides tell us we can't live together. We can live together. You must not believe the lie."

Cecilie Surasky is the Communications Director for Jewish Voice for Peace and a New Voices fellow with the Academy of Educational Development.

ARTICLE 3

NO, IT'S NOT ANTI-SEMITIC

Judith Butler

London Review of Books, 21 August 2003

> Profoundly anti-Israel views are increasingly finding support in progressive intellectual communities. Serious and thoughtful people are advocating and taking actions that are anti-semitic in their effect if not their intent.
>
> —*Lawrence Summers, 17 September 2002*

When the president of Harvard University declared that to criticise Israel at this time and to call on universities to divest from Israel are 'actions that are anti-semitic in their effect, if not their intent,' he introduced a distinction between effective and intentional anti-semitism that is controversial at best. The counter-charge has been that in making his statement, Summers has struck a blow against academic freedom, in effect, if not in intent. Although he insisted that he meant nothing censorious by his remarks, and that he is in favour of Israeli policy being 'debated freely and civilly,' his words have had a chilling effect on political discourse. Among those actions which he called 'effectively anti-semitic' were European boycotts of Israel, anti-globalisation rallies at which criticisms of Israel were voiced, and fund-raising efforts for organisations of 'questionable political provenance'. Of local concern to him, however, was a divestment petition drafted by MIT and Harvard faculty members who oppose Israel's current occupation and its treatment of Palestinians. Summers asked why Israel was being 'singled out . . . among all nations' for a divestment campaign, suggesting that the singling out was evidence of anti-semitic intentions. And though he claimed that aspects of Israel's 'foreign and defence' policy 'can be and should be vigorously challenged,' it was unclear how such challenges could or would take place without being construed as anti-Israel, and why these policy issues, which include occupation, ought not to be vigorously challenged through a divestment campaign. It would seem that calling for divestment is something other than a legitimately 'vigorous challenge,' but we are not given any criteria by which to adjudicate between vigorous challenges that should be articulated, and those which carry the 'effective' force of anti-semitism.

Summers is right to voice concern about rising anti-semitism, and every progressive person ought to challenge anti-semitism vigorously wherever it occurs. It seems, though, that historically we have now reached a position in which Jews cannot legitimately be understood always and only as presumptive victims. Sometimes we surely are, but sometimes we surely are not. No political ethics can start from the assumption that Jews monopolise the position of victim. 'Victim' is a quickly transposable term: it can shift from minute to minute, from the Jew killed by suicide bombers on a bus to the Palestinian child killed by Israeli gunfire. The public sphere needs to be one in which both kinds of violence are challenged insistently and in the name of justice.

If we think that to criticise Israeli violence, or to call for economic pressure to be put on the Israeli state to change its policies, is to be 'effectively anti-semitic,' we will fail to voice our opposition for fear of being named as part of an anti-semitic enterprise. No label could be worse for a Jew, who knows that, ethically and politically, the position with which it would be unbearable to identify is that of the anti-semite. The ethical framework within which most progressive Jews operate takes the form of the following question: will we be silent (and thereby collaborate with illegitimately violent power), or will we make our voices heard (and be counted among those who did what they could to stop that violence), even if speaking poses a risk? The current Jewish critique of Israel is often portrayed as insensitive to Jewish suffering, past as well as present, yet its ethic is based on the experience of suffering, in order that suffering might stop.

Summers uses the 'anti-semitic' charge to quell public criticism of Israel, even as he explicitly distances himself from the overt operations of censorship. He writes, for instance, that 'the only antidote to dangerous ideas is strong alternatives vigorously advocated.' But how does one vigorously advocate the idea that the Israeli occupation is brutal and wrong, and Palestinian self-determination a necessary good, if the voicing of those views calls down the charge of anti-semitism?

To understand Summers's claim, we have to be able to conceive of an effective anti-semitism, one that pertains to certain speech acts. Either it follows on certain utterances, or it structures them, even if that is not the conscious intention of those making them. His view assumes that such utterances will be taken by others as anti-semitic, or received within a given context as anti-semitic. So we have to ask what context Summers has in mind when he makes his claim; in what context is it the case that any criticism of Israel will be taken to be anti-semitic?

It may be that what Summers was effectively saying is that the only way a criticism of Israel can be heard is through a certain acoustic frame, such that the criticism, whether it is of the West Bank settlements, the closing of Birzeit and Bethlehem University, the demolition of homes in Ramallah or Jenin, or the killing of numerous children and civilians, can only be interpreted as showing hatred for Jews. We are asked to conjure a listener who attributes an intention to the speaker: so-and-so has made a public statement against the Israeli occupation, and this must mean that so-and-so hates Jews or is willing to fuel those who do. The criticism is thus given a hidden meaning, one that is at odds with its explicit claim. The criticism of Israel is nothing more than a cloak for that hatred, or a cover for a call for discriminatory action against Jews. In other words, the only way to understand effective anti-semitism is to presuppose intentional anti-semitism; the effective anti-semitism of any criticism turns out to reside in the intention of the speaker as retrospectively attributed by the listener.

It may be that Summers has something else in mind; namely, that the criticism will be exploited by those who want to see not only the destruction of Israel but the degradation or devaluation of Jewish people in general. There is always that risk, but to claim that such criticism of Israel can be taken only as criticism of Jews is to attribute to that particular interpretation the power to monopolise the field of reception. The argument against letting criticism of Israel into the public sphere would be that it gives fodder to those with anti-semitic intentions, who will successfully co-opt the criticism. Here again, a statement can become effectively anti-semitic only if there is, somewhere, an intention to use it for anti-semitic purposes. Indeed, even if one believed that criticisms of Israel are by and large heard as anti-semitic (by Jews, anti-semites, or people who could be described as neither), it would become the responsibility of all of us to change the conditions of reception so that the public might begin to distinguish between criticism of Israel and a hatred of Jews.

Summers made his statement as president of an institution which is a symbol of academic prestige in the United States, and although he claimed he was speaking not as president of the university but as a 'member of our community,' his speech carried weight in the press precisely because he was exercising the authority of his office. If the president of Harvard is letting the public know that he will take any criticism of Israel to be effectively anti-semitic, then he is saying that public discourse itself ought to be so constrained that such statements are not uttered, and that those who utter them will be understood as engaging in anti-semitic speech, even hate speech.

Here, it is important to distinguish between anti-semitic

speech which, say, produces a hostile and threatening environment for Jewish students—racist speech which any university administrator would be obliged to oppose and regulate—and speech which makes a student uncomfortable because it opposes a particular state or set of state policies that he or she may defend. The latter is a political debate, and if we say that the case of Israel is different, that any criticism of it is considered as an attack on Israelis, or Jews in general, then we have singled out this political allegiance from all other allegiances that are open to public debate. We have engaged in the most outrageous form of 'effective' censorship.

The point is not only that Summers's distinction between effective and intentional anti-semitism cannot hold, but that the way it collapses in his formulation is precisely what produces the conditions under which certain public views are taken to be hate speech, in effect if not in intent. Summers didn't say that anything that Israel does in the name of self-defence is legitimate and ought not to be questioned. I don't know whether he approves of all Israeli policies, but let's imagine, for the sake of argument, that he doesn't. And I don't know whether he has views about, for instance, the destruction of homes and the killings of children in Jenin which attracted the attention of the United Nations last year but was not investigated as a human rights violation because Israel refused to open its borders to an investigative team. If he objects to those actions, and they are among the 'foreign policy' issues he believes ought to be 'vigorously challenged,' he would be compelled, under his formulation, not to voice his disapproval, believing, as he does, that that would be construed, effectively, as anti-semitism. And if he thinks it possible to voice disapproval, he hasn't shown us how to do it in such a way as to avert the allegation of anti-semitism.

Summers's logic suggests that certain actions of the Israeli state must be allowed to go on unimpeded by public protest, for fear that any protest would be tantamount to anti-semitism, if not anti-semitism itself. Now, all forms of anti-semitism must be opposed, but we have here a set of serious confusions about the forms anti-semitism takes. Indeed, if the charge of anti-semitism is used to defend Israel at all costs, then its power when used against those who do discriminate against Jews—who do violence to synagogues in Europe, wave Nazi flags or support anti-semitic organisations—is radically diluted. Many critics of Israel now dismiss all claims of anti-semitism as 'trumped up,' having been exposed to their use as a way of censoring political speech.

Summers doesn't tell us why divestment campaigns or other forms of public protest are anti-semitic. According to him, some forms of anti-semitism are characterised as such retroactively, which means that nothing should be said or done that will then be taken to be anti-semitic by others. But what if those others are wrong? If we take one form of anti-semitism to be defined retroactively, what is left of the possibility of legitimate protest against a state, either by its own population or anyone else? If we say that every time the word 'Israel' is spoken, the speaker really means 'Jews,' then we have foreclosed in advance the possibility that the speaker really means 'Israel'. If, on the other hand, we distinguish between anti-semitism and forms of protest against the Israeli state (or right-wing settlers who sometimes act independently of the state), acknowledging that sometimes they do, disturbingly, work together, then we stand a chance of understanding that world Jewry does not see itself as one with Israel in its present form and practice, and that Jews in Israel do not necessarily see themselves as one with the state. In other words, the possibility of a substantive Jewish peace movement depends on our observing a productive and critical distance from the state of Israel (which can be coupled with a profound investment in its future course).

Summers's view seems to imply that criticism of Israel is 'anti-Israel' in the sense that it is understood to challenge the right of Israel to exist. A criticism of Israel is not the same, however, as a challenge to Israel's existence, even if there are conditions under which it would be possible to say that one leads to the other. A challenge to the right of Israel to exist can be construed as a challenge to the existence of the Jewish people only if one believes that Israel alone keeps the Jewish people alive or that all Jews invest their sense of perpetuity in the state of Israel in its current or traditional forms. One could argue, however, that those polities which safeguard the right to criticise them stand a better chance of surviving than those that don't. For a criticism of Israel to be taken as a challenge to the survival of the Jews, we would have to assume not only that 'Israel' cannot change in response to legitimate criticism, but that a more radically democratic Israel would be bad for Jews. This would be to suppose that criticism is not a Jewish value, which clearly flies in the face not only of long traditions of Talmudic disputation, but of all the religious and cultural sources that have been part of Jewish life for centuries.

What are we to make of Jews who disidentify with Israel or, at least, with the Israeli state? Or Jews who identify with Israel, but do not condone some of its practices? There is a wide range here: those who are silently ambivalent about the way Israel handles itself; those who only half articulate their doubts about the occupation; those who are strongly opposed to the occupation, but within a Zionist framework; those who would like to see Zionism rethought or, indeed, abandoned. Jews may hold any of these opinions, but voice them only to their family, or only to their friends; or voice them in public but then face an angry reception at home. Given this Jewish ambivalence, ought we not to be suspicious of any effort to equate Jews with Israel? The argument that all Jews have a heartfelt investment in the state of Israel is untrue. Some have a heartfelt investment in corned beef sandwiches or in certain Talmudic tales, religious rituals and liturgy, in memories of their grandmother, the taste of borscht or the sounds of the old Yiddish theatre. Others have an investment in historical and cultural archives from Eastern Europe or from the Holocaust, or in forms of labour activism, civil rights struggles and social justice that are thoroughly secular, and exist in relative independence from the question of Israel.

What do we make of Jews such as myself, who are emotionally invested in the state of Israel, critical of its current form, and call for a radical restructuring of its economic and juridical basis precisely because we are invested in it? It is always possible to say that such Jews have turned against their own Jewishness. But what if one criticises Israel in the name of one's Jewishness, in the name of justice, precisely because such criticisms seem 'best for the Jews'? Why wouldn't it always be 'best for the Jews' to embrace forms of democracy that extend what is 'best' to everyone, Jewish or not? I signed a petition framed in these terms, an 'Open Letter from American Jews,' in which 3700 American Jews opposed the Israeli occupation, though in my view it was not nearly strong enough: it did not call for the end of Zionism, or for the reallocation of arable land, for rethinking the Jewish right of return or for the fair distribution of water and medicine to Palestinians, and it did not call for the reorganisation of the Israeli state on a more radically egalitarian basis. It was, nevertheless, an overt criticism of Israel.

Many of those who signed that petition will have felt what might reasonably be called heartache at taking a public stand against Israeli policy, at the thought that Israel, by subjecting 3.5 million Palestinians to military occupation, represents the Jews in a way that these petitioners find not only objectionable, but terrible to endure, as Jews; it is as Jews that they assert their disidentification with that policy, that they seek to widen the rift between the state of Israel and the Jewish people in order to produce an alternative vision of the future. The petitioners exercised a democratic right to voice criticism, and sought to get economic pressure put on Israel by the US and other countries, to implement rights for Palestinians otherwise deprived of basic conditions of self-determination, to end the occupation, to secure an independent Palestinian state or to re-establish the basis of the Israeli state without regard to religion so that Jewishness would constitute only one cultural and religious reality, and be protected by the same laws that protect the rights of others.

Identifying Israel with Jewry obscures the existence of the small but important post-Zionist movement in Israel, including the philosophers Adi Ophir and Anat Biletzki, the sociologist Uri Ram, the professor of theatre Avraham Oz and the poet Yitzhak Laor. Are we to say that Israelis who are critical of Israeli policy are self-hating Jews, or insensitive to the ways in which criticism may fan the flames of anti-semitism? What of the new Brit Tzedek organisation in the U.S., numbering close to 20,000 members at the last count, which seeks to offer a critical alternative to the American Israel Political Action Committee, opposing the current occupation and working for a two-state solution? What of Jewish Voice for Peace, Jews against the Occupation, Jews for Peace in the Middle East, the Faculty for Israeli-Palestinian Peace, Tikkun, Jews for Racial and Economic Justice, Women in Black or, indeed, Neve Shalom-Wahat al-Salam, the only village collectively governed by both Jews and Arabs in the state of Israel? What do we make of B'Tselem, the Israeli organisation that monitors human rights abuses in the West Bank and Gaza, or Gush Shalom, an Israeli organisation opposing the occupation, or Yesh Gvul, which represents the Israeli soldiers who refuse to serve in the Occupied Territories? And what of Ta'ayush, a Jewish-Arab coalition against policies that lead to isolation, poor medical care, house arrest, the destruction of educational institutions, and lack of water and food for Palestinians?

It will not do to equate Jews with Zionists or Jewishness with Zionism. There were debates among Jews throughout the 19th and early 20th centuries as to whether Zionism ought to become the basis of a state, whether the Jews had any right to lay claim to land inhabited by Palestinians for centuries, and as to the future for a Jewish political project based on a violent expropriation of land. There were those who sought to make Zionism compatible with peaceful co-existence with Arabs, and those who used it as an excuse for military aggression, and continue to do so. There were those who thought, and still think, that Zionism is not a legitimate basis for a democratic state in a situation where a diverse population must be assumed to practise different religions, and that no group ought to be excluded from any right accorded to citizens in general on the basis of their ethnic or religious views. And there are those who maintain that the violent appropriation of Palestinian land, and the dislocation of 700,000 Palestinians, was an unsuitable foundation on which to build a state. Yet Israel is now repeating its founding gesture in the containment and dehumanisation of Palestinians in the Occupied Territories. Indeed, the wall now being built threatens to leave 95,000 Palestinians homeless. These are questions about Zionism that should and must be asked in a public domain, and universities are surely one place where we might expect critical reflections on Zionism to take place. Instead, we are being asked, by Summers and others, to treat any critical approach to

Zionism as effective anti-semitism and, hence, to rule it out as a topic for legitimate disagreement.

Many important distinctions are elided by the mainstream press when it assumes that there are only two possible positions on the Middle East, the 'pro-Israel' and the 'pro-Palestinian'. The assumption is that these are discrete views, internally homogeneous, non-overlapping, that if one is 'pro-Israel' then anything Israel does is all right, or if 'pro-Palestinian' then anything Palestinians do is all right. But few people's political views occupy such extremes. One can, for instance, be in favour of Palestinian self-determination, but condemn suicide bombings, and find others who share both those views but differ on the form self-determination ought to take. One can be in favour of Israel's right to exist, but still ask what is the most legitimate and democratic form that existence ought to take. If one questions the present form, is one anti-Israel? If one holds out for a truly democratic Israel-Palestine, is one anti-Israel? Or is one trying to find a better form for this polity, one that may well involve any number of possibilities: a revised version of Zionism, a post-Zionist Israel, a self-determining Palestine, or an amalgamation of Israel into a greater Israel-Palestine where all racially and religiously based qualifications on rights and entitlements would be eliminated?

What is ironic is that in equating Zionism with Jewishness, Summers is adopting the very tactic favoured by anti-semites. At the time of his speech, I found myself on a listserv on which a number of individuals opposed to the current policies of the state of Israel, and sometimes to Zionism, started to engage in this same slippage, sometimes opposing what they called 'Zionism' and at other times what they called 'Jewish' interests. Whenever this occurred, there were objections, and several people withdrew from the group. Mona Baker, the academic in Manchester who dismissed two Israeli colleagues from the board of her academic journal in an effort to boycott Israeli institutions, argued that there was no way to distinguish between individuals and institutions. In dismissing these individuals, she claimed, she was treating them as emblematic of the Israeli state, since they were citizens of that country. But citizens are not the same as states: the very possibility of significant dissent depends on recognising the difference between them. Baker's response to subsequent criticism was to submit e-mails to the 'academicsforjustice' listserv complaining about 'Jewish' newspapers and labeling as 'pressure' the opportunity that some of these newspapers offered to discuss the issue in print with the colleagues she had dismissed. She refused to do this and seemed now to be fighting against 'Jews,' identified as a lobby that pressures people, a lobby that had put pressure on her. The criticism that I made of Summers's view thus applies to Baker as well: it is one thing to oppose Israel in its current form and practices or, indeed, to have critical questions about Zionism itself, but it is quite another to oppose 'Jews' or assume that all 'Jews' have the same view, that they are all in favour of Israel, identified with Israel or represented by Israel. Oddly, and painfully, it has to be said that on this point Mona Baker and Lawrence Summers agree: Jews are the same as Israel. In the one instance, the premise works in the service of an argument against anti-semitism; in the second, it works as the effect of anti-semitism itself. One aspect of anti-semitism or, indeed, of any form of racism is that an entire people is falsely and summarily equated with a particular position, view or disposition. To say that all Jews hold a given view on Israel or are adequately represented by Israel or, conversely, that the acts of Israel, the state, adequately stand for the acts of all Jews, is to conflate Jews with Israel and, thereby, to commit an anti-semitic reduction of Jewishness.

In holding out for a distinction to be made between Israel and Jews, I am calling for a space for dissent for Jews, and non-Jews, who have criticisms of Israel to articulate; but I am also opposing anti-semitic reductions of Jewishness to Israeli interests. The 'Jew' is no more defined by Israel than by anti-semitism. The 'Jew' exceeds both determinations, and is to be found, substantively, as a historically and culturally changing identity that takes no single form and has no single telos. Once the distinction is made, discussion of both Zionism and anti-semitism can begin, since it will be as important to understand the legacy of Zionism and to debate its future as to oppose anti-semitism wherever we find it.

What is needed is a public space in which such issues might be thoughtfully debated, and to prevent that space being defined by certain kinds of exclusion and censorship. If one can't voice an objection to violence done by Israel without attracting a charge of anti-semitism, then that charge works to circumscribe the publicly acceptable domain of speech, and to immunise Israeli violence against criticism. One is threatened with the label 'anti-semitic' in the same way that one is threatened with being called a 'traitor' if one opposes the most recent US war. Such threats aim to define the limits of the public sphere by setting limits on the speakable. The world of public discourse would then be one from which critical perspectives would be excluded, and the public would come to understand itself as one that does not speak out in the face of obvious and illegitimate violence.

(Reprinted with the author's permission.)
Judith Butler's book of essays, *Precarious Life: Politics, Violence, Mourning,* about culture and politics after 11 September, is due from Verso in the spring of 2004. She is Maxine Elliot Professor in Rhetoric and Comparative Literature at the University of California at Berkeley. Professor Butler is a member of the Advisory Board of Jewish Voice for Peace.

ARTICLE 4

WHAT IS "ANTI-SEMITISM" AND DOES IT STILL EXIST?

Terry Fletcher

One afternoon last August I tuned into my local progressive community radio station for a program on what I thought would be an interesting topic: false accusations of anti-Semitism from right-wing Jewish organizations that attempt to silence any criticism of Israeli policies. Much to my surprise, one of the first things I heard from the main guest, a left-wing journalist whose work I had previously admired, was that there was no anti-Semitism in the US.

I found this remark shocking, especially coming from a Gentile. How would he know? Would the station put a man on the air to proclaim that there was no sexism? But this journalist had gone on the air with a Jew who seemed to agree with his assertions, and the Jewish host of the program said nothing to challenge them. As outraged and disturbed as I was, I could also understand how these Jews could believe that there was no anti-Semitism. Many years ago I felt the same way.

As I was growing up in California in the 1960s and 70s, my Jewish immigrant parents made every effort to raise us as assimilated "Americans," not as Jews. Their Jewish childhoods hadn't gone well and they thought they would be doing us kids a favor by raising us as "normal Americans" who would easily fit into US culture. We celebrated Easter and Christmas, but no Jewish holidays. We never went near a synagogue or Jewish community center. No Jewish language or expressions were used at home, and we ate "American," not Jewish food.

When, at one point during my college years, I had a Jewish roommate who talked about Jews being an oppressed people, I was amazed. I knew all about the Holocaust, but that had happened on another continent and ended long before I was born. I had never been physically attacked, discriminated against in employment, education or housing; I didn't see large numbers of Jews living in poverty or being exploited at low-wage jobs. Jews didn't seem to get beaten or killed by the police the way Blacks and Latinos were, and there didn't seem to be disproportionate numbers of Jews in prison. "She's nuts!" I thought of my roommate. "Her father's a doctor; what's she got to complain about?"

It wasn't until I began to explore and reclaim my own Jewish identity that I began to understand what my roommate had meant. In my 30s I joined a Jewish folk chorus, went to synagogue a few times, and started lighting candles and engaging in some modicum of Shabbat observance on Friday nights. I stopped celebrating Christmas and started celebrating Chanukah and Passover.

As a teacher, I had just begun a new job in a Berkeley public school. At a staff meeting in early December, I was told that the PTA was going to put on a "holiday" event for the families and students, and that all staff were expected to attend. The event was scheduled for a Friday evening. I wrote an open letter to the PTA in which I said that, as a Jew who honored Shabbat, I could not attend a work event on a Friday night, and that I hoped they could accommodate me and the few Jewish families at the school by changing the date. I said that if the date were not changed, I regretted that I would not be able to attend the event.

The date was not changed and soon I began to receive unpleasant comments from many of my co-workers. One Gentile co-worker told me that I didn't understand what Shabbat was all about and that, once the candles were lit at sundown, I could do anything I wanted. Other co-workers told me that since I didn't keep kosher, it was hypocritical of me not to work on a Friday night. Others challenged my sincerity and accused me of using my religion as an excuse. No one supported me.

I soon began to understand that the reason I hadn't experienced anti-Semitism until then was largely because, for the most part, people didn't know I was Jewish. And even when they did know I was Jewish, the fact that I tried to act like a Gentile made it easy for them to accept me. I'm sure that the goal of my parents' strategy in attempting to raise me to act Gentile was for me to not have to experience the overt anti-Semitism they faced as children, and, for the most part, it worked. But as an adult, I found that the more openly I expressed my Jewish identity, the more I experienced a backlash.

Still, many years later, the anti-Semitism I have personally experienced has come in the form of insensitive and ignorant comments plus the fact that mainstream US culture continues to be dominated by Protestant Christians, making my culture invisible and marginalized. I still have never been physically assaulted (though I know many Jewish men who have), denied employment or housing, forced to live in poverty, beaten by the police, or sent to prison because of my being Jewish. Since we know that these things happen to people of color in the US on a regular basis, what do Jews have to complain about?

The problem with the above comparison is the expectation that anti-Semitism should look like racism, and, if it doesn't, it must not exist, or at least not be as serious a problem. In reality no oppression can be compared to another as worse, better or more serious. Anti-Semitism is a unique phenomenon and has always been different from other forms of oppression. The essence of anti-Semitism is not to keep Jews at the bottom of society, but to set us up as scapegoats to mask the culpability of those really in charge of and responsible for society's ills.

At least since the Middle Ages, ruling classes have successfully deflected people's justifiable anger at their own poverty and oppression by blaming Jews for, among other things, being greedy, controlling, and hoarding all the resources. Though anti-Semitism targets and hurts Jews, its purpose is not to hurt Jews, but to confuse the entire society about who really holds the power and has the resources and control. Therefore a gauge of how much anti-Semitism is taking place is not how badly Jews are faring, but how confused society is as a whole about the real relationships of power.

Through much of European history, Jews were forbidden to own land or work at most respectable jobs. Among the few jobs Jews were allowed to perform were money lending and tax collecting. While a few Jews were able to make a good living at these jobs, the vast majority lived in poverty, as did most Gentiles. Yet when people became angry at having to pay so many taxes, it was easy for the local ruler to point to "the Jews" and their greediness as the problem while he continued to hold the real power and wealth of the society.

This same dynamic is alive and well today. When people around the world justifiably protest US support for Israel's oppressive policies or the war in Iraq, it is very convenient for those really behind these policies to blame them on the Jewish lobby. But what would US policy look like were it not for AIPAC? Probably like US policy in Central America, Columbia, Chile, the Philippines, Vietnam and Cuba.

US society and the global economy really are controlled by a small group of people that includes a few Jews, but for the most part is made up of Protestants of European heritage. US policies, domestic and foreign, are based on what these people think their interests are. As a result, the US has quite often stood on the side of oppressive regimes and against justice and self-determination for oppressed people. Yet only when it comes to the Middle East do many believe that the cause is not US attempts at world domination, but the influence of a lobby. US policy on Israel/Palestine is not an anomaly.

Confronting anti-Semitism can be very difficult and painful for progressive Jews. Though Jews in the US come from all economic and social backgrounds, anti-Semitism says that we are rich, powerful and privileged, so we are often perceived in this way, even on the Left. In general, for the last few decades, the US Left has not regarded anti-Semitism as an important issue to address and has treated it as non-existent or unimportant. Many of us have internalized these ideas and feel as if we have no right to bring up our own mistreatment when others, such as the Palestinians, are suffering so much more.

One thing I try to remember when confronting anti-Semitism is that it is often less harmful to me and other Jews than it is to the person or group directing it at us. Having any kind of oppression operating from within a social change movement, be it racism, sexism, homophobia or anti-Semitism, makes that movement less powerful by marginalizing some of its members and potential allies, thereby both excluding their much-needed perspectives and creating painful divisions. Even more importantly, for a social change movement to be effective, it must have a clear analysis of the actual dynamic of power that is responsible for creating the situation it is trying to change. This is where anti-Semitism traditionally and currently has been used to confuse people by blaming Jews rather than those who are really in power.

So what can we Jews do about anti-Semitism? The good news is that there are steps we can take. Like many other oppressions, anti-Semitism relies on misinformation. The more people actually get to know us as people, the less they will be able to believe these lies. So we can do a lot to combat anti-Semitism just by reaching out to non-Jews, forming good relationships, providing good information and acting in a principled way. We should then call on these allies to help us combat anti-Semitism, and expect them to do this well.

Progressive Jews and our allies need to recognize and confront anti-Semitism where we see it. After all, getting rid of anti-Semitism will not just help Jews; it is a crucial step in the transformation of our world into one in which there is peace and justice for all peoples.

Terry Fletcher is a public elementary school teacher, a union activist, and the daughter of a Holocaust survivor. She has been active with Jewish Voice for Peace since 1999.

ARTICLE 5

BOGUS CHARGES
Henri Picciotto

Inevitably in the discussions of Iraq, the question of Israel-Palestine comes up. This is not surprising—the issues are related, and deserve vigorous discussion both separately and together. During the buildup to the war such discussion happened, but unfortunately, at the slightest hint of criticism of Israeli policies, some people responded with charges of anti-Semitism.

Sometimes there is merit to these charges. The claim that "the Jews" are the cause of war on Iraq is a rehashing of a classical anti-Semitic shibboleth about Jews running everything. Unfortunately, we hear this sort of thing increasingly often, not only from the right, but also from progressives who have seemingly lost perspective: yes, the pro-Israel lobby (which involves Christian fundamentalists as well as Jews,) is powerful, but United States Middle East policy is primarily set according to the geo-political concerns of the US establishment, not the demands of any one lobby.

The claim that it is somehow wrong to involve leaders of the Jewish community in the anti-war coalition is a sign that some activists were falling for a classical divide-and-conquer form of anti-Semitism. Fortunately, in the Bay Area anyway, this point of view was soundly defeated. Many Jews played a leadership role, as Jews, in the anti-war movement, and several rabbis and Jewish peace activists spoke at the rallies. This included Jewish Voice for Peace's co-Director and the rabbi of the largest synagogue in San Francisco. This sort of full and visible Jewish participation is the best way to oppose actual anti-Semitism in a principled and uncompromising way. We also expect from our allies in the anti-war movement and in the progressive movement to speak out and support us on this issue.

However, charges of anti-Semitism sometimes are simply bogus.

Bogus charge: "It is anti-Semitic to 'bash' Israel at a demonstration about Iraq." This ignores the fact there is a profound link between the US support for the Israeli government and the US war on Iraq. Both have to do with how our government sees its geopolitical interests in the Middle East; both reveal the US government's disregard for the lives of Arabs; and the fog of war distracted the US public from paying attention to the escalated attacks on the Palestinians. It is entirely legitimate for one to draw these connections.

Bogus charge: "It is anti-Semitic to criticize Israel without criticizing other countries that commit atrocities." Not necessarily so! There are many reasons for people to focus on Israeli wrongdoings. Palestinians, for example, have a reason or two to bring this up. Jews also feel a particular association to this conflict. Besides, all Americans have a right to question how our foreign aid dollars are spent. US military aid to Israel is by far the largest given to any country. These billions of dollars a year make us accomplices to the illegal, immoral, and ultimately self-destructive occupation of the West Bank, Gaza Strip, and East Jerusalem.

Bogus charge: "It is anti-Semitic to say that the US government is attacking Iraq in part because of its strategic alliance with Israel." This statement should be discussed based on the evidence. It cannot be rejected out of hand on ideological grounds. True, any claim that Israel runs the US government is ridiculous, but it is no secret that many of the neoconservative hawks in Bush's circle are vigorous supporters of Israeli Prime Minister Sharon and his right-wing policies.

Bogus charge: "The antiwar movement must be anti-Semitic because some Jews feel uncomfortable at peace marches." While there are some objectionable signs and speakers at demonstrations, there are other reasons that may account for some of this discomfort. Many Jews are not accustomed to hearing Israel being criticized. Many Jews are not used to contact with Arabs. Some are uncomfortable at the sight of Palestinian flags or demonstrators wearing kaffiyehs (the Palestinian checkered headdress). That particular discomfort is not evidence of anti-Semitism at the march—quite the contrary, it may be symptomatic of an inability among some to acknowledge the humanity of Palestinians and their right to a national identity.

Bogus charge: "It is anti-Semitic to call for 'the liberation of Palestine, from the river to the sea,' or to wear a t-shirt that says 'I hate '48'." Anti-Zionist views are not necessarily anti-Semitic, and they cannot and should not be kept out of the antiwar movement. Likewise, pro-Zionist views are not necessarily racist, and they cannot and should not be kept out of the antiwar movement. At JVP we have agreed that, while we as an organization will not endorse pro- or anti-Zionist views, we do not rule out working with pro- or anti-Zionist individuals and groups. In fact, it is highly unlikely that we can succeed in building a movement against the occupation without working with both pro- and anti-Zionist individuals and groups.

We and our allies should strongly challenge signs and speeches that equate Zionism with Nazism, Sharon with Hitler, and the Star of David with the swastika. The comparison is inaccurate and offensive. Unfortunately, it has become increasingly common as the Israeli government continues its disastrous policy of occupation and repression. When the Israeli military kills children, demolishes houses, uproots olive trees, steals water, bombs apartment buildings, commits assassinations, imposes round-the-clock curfews, and humiliates an entire people, it is inevitable someone will speak out against it, and not only in the ways that we would.

For decades, some leaders of the Jewish community have made the preposterous claim that there is complete unity of belief and interest between all Jews and the Israeli government no matter what its policies. They must believe their own propaganda, because they see no difference between criticism of the Israeli government and anti-Semitism, and they do everything they can to silence critical voices. If the brand of anti-Semitism is not sufficiently intimidating, the silencing has been enforced by organized phone and letter-writing campaigns, boycotts, threats of and actual withdrawal of funding support from "offending" institutions and individuals.

This must change. Because of our government's deep and one-sided involvement in the region, the Israel-Palestine conflict will not be resolved without extensive dialogue here in the US. This dialogue must, of necessity, involve Jews and Arabs, Zionists and anti-Zionists, people who love Israel and people who love Palestine. We must listen to all those voices and oppose the relentless and anti-democratic attempts to silence some of them.

Henri Picciotto is a mathematics teacher, a Jew from Lebanon, and a long-time Berkeley resident. He is a member of the Coordinating Committee of Jewish Voice for Peace.

ARTICLE 6

DISCRIMINATION, RACISM AND ANTI-SEMITISM IN OUR COMMUNITY

Laurie Polster

When one speaks of anti-Semitism, it is impossible not to make the broader link to discrimination, intolerance, and racism in general. For anti-Semitism—in its most commonly understood definition as bias or hatred against Jews—cannot be disconnected from societal intolerance and hatred, whether religiously or ethnically based, directed from the outside or internally centered.

The bombing of a synagogue is a morally indefensible criminal act of hatred, in the same unquestionable terms as is the burning of a black church or the physical destruction of a mosque or a Hindu house of prayer. Verbal or physical attacks against a person, institution, or community solely because of his, her, or its Jewishness is anti-Semitic, and it must be denounced from all sectors of society with the same vehemence and outrage as all identity-based hatred. One can be no more or no less outraged by one act of intolerance or another directed at any identity group, for each attack is, at its core, an attack on the basic respect, human dignity, and human rights of every individual.

Recently, leaders of the mainstream Jewish community have written and spoken about a rise in anti-Semitism. This is expressed first as a primal need for the Jewish people to be increasingly vigilant in the face of potential annihilation,

• REFRAMING ANTI-SEMITISM •

and to uphold Israel's existence and security as paramount to Jewish survival, to insure that another Holocaust will never happen. Many remember that their countries were either insensitive or outright complicit to the plight of European Jews during the mid-1930s to 1948, during the rise of Nazism and the extermination of 6 million Jews in German death camps. Many remember the refusal to resettle Jewish survivors of the war within their own countries, or (in the case of Britain) to allow for Jewish immigration to Palestine before Israel declared itself a state in May 1948.

This concern and outcry is both understandable and necessary. However, it rings hollow and hypocritical without a simultaneous reflection and outcry over the discrimination and racism emanating within Jewish society. Some of it is directed towards Arabs in general (whether Palestinian, Bedouin and Druze citizens of Israel, towards Palestinian residents of the Occupied Territories or Arabs more generally) and some of it is directed against Jews by other Jews, evidenced in the institutionalized Ashkenazi (European Jewish) racism against the Mizrahim (Jews originating from Arab and Muslim countries).

If one travels throughout Israel today, it is impossible not to notice—unless you cannot read Hebrew—numerous publicly painted pieces of graffiti which read: "Death to the Arabs," and "Kill the Arabs." That hatemongers exist in any society who would publicly display such invective is one thing. That the public outcry within Israel and the worldwide Jewish community against such public displays is so mute that this graffiti is not removed within moments of its appearance and emphatically denounced speaks volumes. One can only imagine the outcry from these same Jewish leaders if graffiti were emblazoned across several communities throughout America (or anywhere else in the world for that matter) with the words, "Death to the Jews," and " Kill All the Jews."

A more scathing indictment manifests itself in the institutionalized discrimination of Israeli Arab citizens, who comprise over a million people, one sixth of Israel's population. In all areas of housing, education, employment, infrastructure development to communities, and contact with authorities, Israeli government support and treatment of its Arab citizens and their communities is so abysmally substandard and disproportionately inadequate compared to that of its Jewish population, that it cannot be seen as anything other than overt racism and discrimination. In a landmark decision on September 1, 2003, an Israeli commission of inquiry accused the police of excessive force three years ago, which resulted in the death of 13 Israeli-Arabs who were demonstrating in solidarity with the intifada, "...while combating riots it said resulted from simmering, overlooked anger at the Israeli establishment's widespread discrimination against Israeli Arabs. It criticized police tactics and concluded that Israel must educate its police that the Arab public is not the enemy, and should not be treated as such." (New York Times, September 2, 2003).

Equally appalling and less widely known, is the racism directed against Mizrahi Jews from the Ashkenazi oligarchy establishment, which founded the Zionist movement and has dominated and controlled the Israeli government and all of Israel's main institutions, including the military, education, and economic sectors since pre-Israel Palestine. Since Zionism was a direct response to European Christian anti-Semitism, it was primarily a European Jewish movement. Historically, Jews living in Arab countries pre-1948 were for the most part secure within their respected communities, integrated into the prevailing culture and societies, with little or no interest in immigration to Palestine. Their centuries-old longing for a return to Zion was a cultural/religious desire and not a nationalist movement. That many second and third generation Mizrahi Jews have become subsequent supporters of right-wing Likud policies needs to be viewed in the context of an anti-establishment vote, a legacy of total rejection by the Ashkenazi Labor party which actually represents the ruling oligarchy.

Whether in British mandated Palestine or under the newly formed State of Israel, Jewish discourse and government policies have been riddled with discrimination against Mizrahi Jews. These attitudes were clearly delineated in the words of Nahum Goldman, Chair of the World Zionist Organization, "A European Jew is worth twice more than a Kurdish Jew." Under David Ben Gurion, the founding Prime Minister of Israel, most state lands confiscated from Palestinians in 1948, including the kibbutzim, were consigned to the sole control of Ashkenazi Jews. Currently most agricultural land is controlled by 3% of the population, basically the kibbutzim and Ashkenazi farmers like Prime Minister Ariel Sharon. A mainstay of the Zionist-

Labor movement, the kibbutzim were heavily subsidized by the Israeli government in the form of land, equipment, infrastructure, seed, fertilizer and other material needs. In comparison, newly arrived Judeo-Arab refugees—who lost everything when they emigrated—were initially placed in tent camps where they often languished for years. (In the case of the Iraqi Jews, they were actually deloused upon their airplane arrival into the Promised Land). They were then transferred to border communities to act as a buffer to the Arab 'enemy' whom they were culturally connected to, or placed in industrial development towns to become the underclass workers of the new state. When the Iron Curtain dropped and effectively curtailed Jewish immigration from Eastern Europe, Jews from Arab countries were lured to Israel for the express purpose of being laborers. PM David Ben Gurion summed it up nicely, "We need people who are workers from birth. We should pay attention to local Mizrahim."

Mizrahi children were given substandard education and tracked into vocational programs. This furthered socio-economic disparities and perpetuated second-class citizenship into subsequent generations. By the 1970's, 80% of welfare recipients were Mizrahim. 55% of Mizrahi students dropped out of school, the remainder primarily tracked into vocational training, where even today 42% are still tracked.

Unemployment has been the worst disaster for Mizrahim, perpetuating a culture of poverty and welfare. Currently 32% of Mizrahi families live at or below the poverty line. There are more that 300,000 unemployed in Israel, the vast majority Mizrahim. The average Ashkenazi family earns 50% more than a Mizrahi family, and 400,000 Mizrahi children live in poverty. Not unlike what has happened within minority communities in America, the dead-end cycle of marginally addressed and institutionalized poverty, inferior education, and unemployment has led to a high incidence of drug addiction and crime. Currently there are 250,000 drug addicts in Israel, mostly Mizrahim. Of the prison population, 90% are Mizrahim.

In 1971 the Israeli Black Panthers—initially a small group of disenfranchised Mizrahi youth from the Musrara neighborhood in Jerusalem—burst onto the scene in demonstrations and actions protesting the severe poverty and social injustice. Their actions quickly drew thousands of supporters from across the country and nearly toppled the Labor government of PM Golda Meir. When the Panthers applied for a legal permit to hold a large demonstration, the Israeli government tried to suppress the protest by arresting members in the middle of the night, one by one. Golda Meir issued orders to Mosad and the police, who used methods not unlike totalitarian regimes to break up the Panther organization. (One should note with irony that at the same time Jews were decrying Soviet methods of repression against dissent.) What finally halted the protests was the 1973 Yom Kippur War.

Whenever social and security issues have competed in Israel, security has completely dominated the political agenda and thwarted most attempts to unmask the systemic racism and discrimination, which would necessarily force a socio-political overhaul. The Mizrahi and Palestinian struggles are intertwined, and members of the Panthers realized this early on, meeting with members of the PLO in 1972 to address their mutual desire to end the Occupation. Ella Shohat, a noted feminist and academic whose family lived in Baghdad writes, "My grandmother, who still lives in Israel and still communicates largely in Arabic, had to be taught to speak of "us" as Jews and "them" as Arabs. For Middle Easterners, the operating distinction had always been "Muslim," "Jew," and "Christian," not Arab versus Jew. The assumption was that "Arabness" referred to a common shared culture and language, albeit with religious differences."

Today we have arrived at a juncture where the desire to erase "Arabness" from Jewish culture and identity—except in the chic and appropriated forms of ethnic food, aspects of costume and dress, and world music—is both accepted and institutionally supported. Overt racism against Arabs is endemic to Israeli, and by extension Diaspora Jewish society. Only when worldwide Jewry acknowledges, addresses and redresses its own racism, will it establish itself a place of moral integrity within the world community, to effectively challenge and condemn the ongoing legacy of anti-Semitism and to prevent its resurgence.

Laurie Polster is an artist, singer, arts educator, and activist, and a member of Jewish Voice for Peace. She is currently engaged in research and development of a project that re-frames Arab Jewish identity and the cultural and socio-political relationships between Jews and Arabs.

Some of the quotes, facts, and figures in this article were taken from the documentary film *The (Israeli) Black Panthers Speak,* by Israeli filmmaker Sami Shalom Chetrit, PhD.

ARTICLE 7

HISTORICAL U.S. ANTI-SEMITISM— THE INVISIBLE OPPRESSION:
STEREOTYPING, SCAPEGOATING, DISCOUNTING
Penny Rosenwasser

Introduction
As charges of anti-Semitism are hurled by segments of the Jewish community in response to critiques of Israeli government policies—just as anti-Semitic incidents have increased since 9/11—how many of us are aware of what anti-Semitism has looked like in this country: where it has shown up, when, and how? By no means a comprehensive examination, this brief overview highlights major patterns and areas of historical anti-Semitism in the United States—from stereotypes to scapegoating, quotas to a federal cover-up, physical violence to anti-Semitism on the Left. It's a story of bias and racism and Jewish vulnerability—and Jewish resilience.

The Creation Of Jewish Stereotypes
Negative stereotyping of Jews, just because they were Jews, was carried over from Europe and became a key manifestation of anti-Semitism in the United States. As early as 1836, the elementary textbook well-known to so many schoolchildren—the McGuffy Reader—portrayed Jews as greedy, sly, wicked, crafty, selfish, dishonest and unethical. Of course, the most hideous charge was that Jews killed Christ and continued to use Christian children's blood for Jewish rituals—charges compounded by Jewish refusal to repent or

convert. Underlying the stereotypes was the belief that Jews were enemies of Christians, and were a people to be hated and feared. Jews have unfortunately internalized these attitudes, resulting in feelings of fear and self-hatred.

Despite the fact that Sephardic Jews arrived in the Americas with Columbus, Jews have consistently been targeted as "alien" and "different" in this country (though Jews are not the only ones treated this way). Such prejudices have stayed under the surface during periods of calm, but in crises, Jews have often been feared as outsiders. For example, Mark Twain wrote about Jews, "You will always be by ways and habit and predilections substantially strangers—foreigners—wherever you are, and that will probably keep the race prejudice against you alive." That's one of many attitudes Jews have had to face here.

Just before the climax of US anti-Semitism in the late 1930's-1940's, a 1938 public opinion poll shows that 60% of those responding saw Jews as aggressive, greedy and dishonest. By 1942, 42% of Americans polled said they did not want Jews moving into their neighborhood, second only to "Negroes"; and in 1946, when asked "Have you heard any criticism of Jews in the last six months?," 64% of those polled replied "Yes."

The Stereotype Of 'Jewish Power'

Of all the degrading stereotypes about Jews, the "Jewish power" stereotype is particularly potent. It is complicated by the realities that many US Jews have gained some measure of economic, social, and/or political power, while a much smaller percentage are poverty-stricken. But it is a stereotype far older than present-day United States, and it stems from the anti-Semitic dynamic, which is also the nature of stereotyping, of branding an entire group with what may be true for one or two individuals—of targeting The Jew, and ignoring the powerful majority who are not Jewish. For example, in this country's history, some Jews have controlled a few major industries, but have been absent in (and perhaps even excluded from) many others. Is this truly Jewish "power"?

The time period 1938-1945 illustrates the complexities behind the "Jewish power" stereotype. According to polls of the period, almost 45% of the US population believed that Jews had "too much power" in commerce, business and finance—and in fact, some Jews in the 1930's owned most of New York City's factories, retail and wholesale establishments. Yet most Jews at this time were on the brink of poverty. In 1936, the Forbes magazine survey showed that Jewish executives were represented in the textile, film and broadcasting industries—but were actually absent in the finance industry, as well as in insurance, steel, utilities, railroads and autos.

The more visible Jews have become in the economy and in government, the more they are targeted. Yet their attackers have also been condemned. When American hero Charles Lindbergh lambasted Jews in 1941, claiming "Their greatest danger….lies in their large ownership and influence in our motion pictures, our press, our radio and our government," 93% of newspapers condemned Lindbergh's comments, along with protest from church and political leaders.

The irony is that although Jews at this time were perceived as powerful, in truth they had little influence; as many have noted, if Jews had had real power, they would have been able to pressure the US to admit Jewish refugees fleeing Hitler and to intervene in the death camps.

In another example of the anti-Semitic dynamic of focusing on positions where Jews have gained systemic power, and ignoring those areas where Jews are not represented, an American Jewish Committee survey in the mid-1970's showed one Jew among 377 senior banking executives. Yet in 1981, 43% of Americans polled believed that Jews controlled international banking and 37% thought Jews had too much power in the business world. Senator William Proxmire argued that "No industry has more consistently and cruelly rejected Jews from positions of power and influence than commercial banking."

In terms of documenting recent Jewish economic success, Jewish sociologist Riv-Ellen Prell has reported estimates that 25% of the Forbes 400 List for the year 2000 were Jews. Most Jews live in a few large states which control almost half of the Electoral College, Jews contribute up to half of Democratic campaign funds, Jewish representation in Congress has tripled, and Orthodox Jew Joseph Lieberman almost became Vice-President in the last presidential election. The National Jewish Population Study (2001-2003) reports that "more than 60% of all employed Jews are in one of the three highest status job categories;" the current median income of Jewish households is $54,000, as compared to the median US household income of $42,000.

This shows that anti-Semitism has not kept Jews from being allowed to prosper economically en masse or to achieve political power—just as economic prosperity does not mean that Jews are no longer targeted or blamed in hurtful and demeaning ways.

In fact, because anti-Semitism is no longer an economic oppression in this country, many people refuse to take it seriously, and it has become an invisible oppression. Meanwhile, a 2003 study by United Jewish Appeal-Federation showed that one in five Jews living in New York City are living in poverty, many of whom are aging Jews, single mothers, and/or Russian immigrants.

Clearly, Jews have achieved a measure of economic, social and political power—and even disproportionate power in a few industries, relative to their percentage of the US population. It is also true that the vast majority of institutional power in this country is still held by non-Jews. Jewish activist and author Paul Kivel points out how one of the ways that anti-Semitism works is that "we are encouraged to see Jews more visibly than white Christians, so that our attention never quite focuses on the white Christian leadership of our government and corporations– so the economic roots of injustice remain unscathed." That is, there tends to be much more focus on any one Jew who has a modicum of power, than on the majority of powerful non-Jews in any corporate boardroom, nonprofit organization, or governmental body.

Categorizing the current US ruling class as about 1% of the population, or 2.7 million people, with incomes beginning at $370,000/year and minimal net worths of $2,045,000, Kivel also explains that "there is a higher percentage of Jews in the ruling class [for example, the heads of Dupont, Disney and Bank of America], than their representation in the general population, but despite the stereotypes, they still constitute a very small part of that class." The top 20% of the population—which includes the top 1% (above) and the managerial class who implement ruling class policies—are "primarily white and Christian, although there are certainly distinct minorities of people of color, Jews" and others." Even so, as recently as 1990, 21% of Christian Americans believed Jews had too much power in business.

So the "Jewish Power" and "Jewish Money" stereotypes actually serve to keep the focus on the small number of Jews who are part of the owning class, rather than on the predominantly Christian nature of the US owning class. By singling out Jews as scapegoats, instead of focusing on those who are making decisions at the highest levels, anti-Semitism masks what is really class antagonism.

As Kivel points out:

> "Whenever the stereotypes of Jewish money or power go unchallenged, the injustice of our economic system is strengthened and racism is continued. Blaming Jewish bankers or African-American women on welfare are parallel strategies to divert our attention from the corporate elite that makes the economic decisions that affect our lives. These strategies give the majority of white people the mistaken impression that they are controlled by Jews

and in competition with people of color—squeezed on both sides."

Stereotypes Which Target Jewish Women—from the Gentile and Jewish Communities

Various Jewish feminist writers point out the stereotypes created by Jewish men, and then adopted by the rest of society, which demean Jewish women. Although not excusable, it is a way that Jewish men have responded to the anti-Semitism directed at them, by then projecting it onto Jewish women. Riv-Ellen Prell explains that "Gentiles blamed Jews, and Jews blamed Jewish women."

The "Jewish Mother" stereotype is an example of such misogyny. As Jews were allowed to become upwardly mobile after World War II, as a result of the benefits of the GI Bill of Rights (the 1944 Serviceman's Readjustment Act), Jewish mothers were blamed for all the feelings of anxiety and ambivalence brought up by assimilation into middle-class whiteness. The Jewish mother was mocked as a perversion of Jewish love and strength—as being too powerful, manipulative, suffocating, needy, and nurturing—and as dominating Jewish husbands and sons into silence. This also fit into the general "mother-bashing" mode of the 1950's, exemplified by Dr. Spock.

Of course the J.A.P., or "Jewish American Princess," is a horrific example of the culmination of misogyny against Jewish women—a stereotype seemingly created by Jewish men but perpetuated by non-Jews. Seen as young, affluent, materialistic, entitled, and obnoxious, she is targeted as deviant and undesirable, with endless needs—and has been particularly attacked on college campuses, where football crowds have screamed "J.A.P.!" when certain young women walk by. One theory is that the "J.A.P." was created by a culture of consumers who needed to blame their own materialistic excesses on some distinct group. Jewish feminist activist and writer Melanie Kaye/Kantrowitz calls the "J.A.P." "a sexist scapegoating of Jewish middle-class women for the crimes of capitalism." Fortunately, Jewish women artists have defied this stereotype by creating women characters who are witty, empowered and independent.

Jews as Scapegoats—Jewish Vulnerability, Jews as Buffers & the "Socialism of Fools"

Even though Jews have been less discriminated against in the US than in Europe—as well as being given new opportunities, and sometimes even being accepted—during economic or societal crises, Jews have often been blamed as the cause of the problem. Still today, Jews who are landlords, small businesspeople, teachers, social workers, doctors, lawyers, managers and government bureaucrats are sometimes attacked for being in positions of control over others, while also serving as the public faces of—or buffers for—the policy-setters and big decision-makers, the sources of institutional power.

Jewish Feelings of Vulnerability

Jews often look like they have power because they are "set up" in intermediary positions between those on the bottom rungs of society and those in charge. The way the scapegoating pattern works is that groups who are visibly oppressed don't see the heads of corporations, they see mid-level Jewish managers, business people and professionals—and they are fed the stereotypes of Jews as controlling Congress, Hollywood and the media. When something goes wrong, people on the lower rungs are then urged to blame Jews, rather than holding those at the top of the ladder responsible. In 1969 James Baldwin described it as the Jew "playing the role assigned him [sic] by Christians long ago; he [sic] is doing their dirty work."

This leads to what is distinctive about anti-Semitism: how Jews often feel very vulnerable to an unpredictable attack (because this has been true historically, as well as in the present), even though from the outside it looks like their position is secure and even powerful. Jews may accept positions in which they are the visible face of those doing the real damage, in an effort to find secure footing.

Evelyn Torton Beck, who wrote the groundbreaking anthology Nice Jewish Girls, suggests that this scapegoating pattern understandably leaves Jews feeling wary and insecure:

> "If at certain moments in history some Jews have entered into the mainstream, it is only because some powerful groups have 'allowed' it: often this is done with the purpose of using Jews as a buffer and/or as an easy scapegoat when one is needed. It is an age-old pattern for Jews—today, allowed in, perhaps even encouraged; tomorrow, ignominiously thrown out. Many people fail to understand the implications of this recurrent fact of Jewish history… refusing to acknowledge the precariousness of Jewish existence. Is that why, even now, I feel I have to

justify my concern? To prove than any form of anti-Semitism is always a real danger?"

Jews are clearly not the only groups scapegoated, in these times of fierce repression against immigrants, welfare mothers, and people who are Muslim or of Arab descent. Along with Jews, Kaye/Kantrowitz points out that Japanese, Koreans, Arabs, Indians and Pakistanis are also branded as "money-grubbing"—while young disenfranchised men of color are blamed for societal problems. "One group is blamed for capitalism's crimes, the other for capitalism's fallout," she observes. "Do I need to point out who escapes all blame?"

Examples of Anti-Semitic Scapegoating in the US

The worst periods of anti-Semitic scapegoating in this country have been during times of economic strain, societal unrest and fear: during the Civil War, the Great Depression, and the period prior to and during World War II.

Just before the Civil War, northern newspapers attacked Jewish financiers as "hooked nose wretches," accusing them of war-profiteering. In 1862 General Ulysses Grant expelled all Jews from his western Tennessee military district following army scandals in which Jews participated but were in the minority; their physical difference visibly marked them, however, and so they were most targeted. President Lincoln later rescinded Grant's order, only to be followed by the Confederate House of Representatives denouncing Jews, while some southern towns expelled Jews for being disloyal and not pro-slavery enough.

• REFRAMING ANTI-SEMITISM •

During the Great Depression, Henry Ford's paper, *The Dearborn Independent*, reprinted in 1920 the mythological "Rabbi's Letter," which supposedly appeared in turn-of-the-century Russia through the czarist secret police. This letter announced a Jewish conspiracy to take over the world and seize all wealth; known as "The Protocols of the Elders of Zion," it was a vicious manifesto based on historic anti-Semitic stereotypes of Jewish power. The Independent published 91 weeks of attacks on Jews, blaming them for controlling US media and banks, and predicting a Jewish take-over of the country—just as Americans were plunged in financial crisis, uncertainty and fear. The paper's circulation skyrocketed in urban working-class and rural areas, just as prominent Americans and journals denounced the manifesto. Although the "Protocols" were eventually exposed as a fraud, they are still in distribution.

From 1933 to 1939, the most virulent Jewish oppression yet in the U.S exploded in response to the economic crisis and the Nazi takeover of power in Germany. Father Charles Coughlin, a charismatic priest with the National Union for Social Justice, drew an unprecedented following from those traumatized by the Depression, mostly from the poor and working classes, by instilling in them fear of a Communist/Jewish takeover. He also blamed Jews for Germany's economic woes, portrayed Hitler as Europe's savior, and minimized the brutal 1938 Kristallnacht attack on Jews in Germany, the most extensive pogrom in history. By 1941 over 100 US anti-Semitic organizations had formed where only a handful existed before.

And as President Roosevelt had opened opportunities for Jews in high office, including Supreme Court Justice Louis Brandeis and Presidential advisor Felix Frankfurter, Jews were blamed for the New Deal, and Roosevelt was accused of selling out the country to the Jews.

Polls of the era testify to the extent of anti-Jewish feeling: in 1938, half of Americans polled held Jews responsible for Hitler's treatment of them, and 45% thought poorly of Jews. By the 1940's, 43% said they would support an anti-Jewish campaign. Riv-Ellen Prell even argues that a greater percentage of Americans had negative attitudes about Jews than about Germans or Japanese with whom the US was at war—and this at a time when Germany was annihilating Jews by the millions. Finally, numerous Jewish (as well as non-Jewish) leftists were attacked as Communists by McCarthyism, brought before the House Un-American Activities Committee, and blacklisted, ruining many lives.

Institutional Jewish Oppression: Doors Slamming Shut

After Sephardic Jews from Spain and Portugal landed here with Columbus, the second largest immigration wave of Jews—primarily Ashkenazi Jews from Central and Western Europe—arrived in the 1840's. A third wave of Jewish immigrants escaping pogroms in Russia and eastern Europe hit American shores in the 1880's, comprising ten percent of the 23 million immigrants who fled here up until 1914.

This established a significant Jewish presence in America, initiating a dynamic that was to continue: increased populations of Jews, or increased Jewish visibility, leading to increased Jewish oppression. Implemented by upper-class

Americans who did not want Jews around, they legislated institutional barriers to keep Jews from infiltrating upper-crust Christian society, effectively excluding Jews from certain private schools, clubs, and resorts—as well as from housing developments and occupations.

Harvard led elite universities in instituting a quota system against Jewish students, to keep them from undermining wealthy Protestant bastions of social distinction, and by 1930 many private eastern schools had followed suit. Of all the new immigrants, the Jews were most repellent, because not only were they not Christian, but it was feared they would take over economic and political power.

Immigration Restrictions on Jews—and anti-Jewish Racism
Although Chinese immigrants were the first to be prohibited because of their nationality, in 1882, by 1924-27 the first massive immigration restrictions in this country limited all Asians and Jews, along with other southern and Eastern European immigrants. The largest allotments were given to (presumably non-Jewish) immigrants from Great Britain, Ireland and Germany.

These restrictions reflected a xenophobic response to economic crisis, compounded by racism and anti-Semitism.

Specifically, in the late 1800's, racial determinism ideas swept through Europe and into the United States by the early 1900's. This pseudo "scientific," or "objective," racism insisted that Jews' biology was inferior, reflecting their moral inferiority, thus justifying their oppression. Austrian journalist Wilhelm Marr, who was one of many scientific intellectuals in Germany who divided the world according to race (and who himself was the son of a Jew who converted) first coined the term "anti-Semitism" in 1873. Jewish Voice for Peace co-Director Mitchell Plitnick explains that "Marr's coining of the phrase intended to establish a new vicious theory as to why Jews are the enemy…and to give the hatred of Jews a more palatable name than "Judenhass."

In America, such scientific racism categorized all immigrants from southern and eastern Europe as racially inferior, not just Jews—though of this group Jews were seen as the major threat to Anglo-Saxon supremacy. Polls from the period reflect these attitudes: despite Nazi Germany's state-sponsored Jewish oppression which began in the early 1930's, by 1938 77% of Americans polled believed that more Jewish refugees from Germany should be barred from entering the US.

In 1939, 66% disagreed with allowing 10,000 Jewish refugee children to immigrate over the US quota limits; and although several Congresspeople proposed bringing over refugee children from Europe, President Roosevelt refused, saying he did not want to alienate popular opinion.

By 1941 very few immigrants were allowed through America's gates, including Jews, and in 1943, 78% of Americans objected to allowing more immigrants into the country after the war. At the end of 1945, when word was out about the disastrous conditions faced by displaced refugees, only 5% supported raising immigration quotas.

The US State Department's Attempted Cover-Up of the "Final Solution"—America's Doors Still Closed

But not only did the US drastically reduce the number of Jewish refugees escaping Hitler who were allowed into the country—the State Department initially tried to cover up word of Hitler's genocide against European Jews.

Holocaust historian Michael Berenbaum exposes the story, which began in early August 1942, when German industrialist Edward Schulte leaked word that Hitler planned to kill all of Europe's Jews—launching his "Final Solution" to the "Jewish problem"—to World Jewish Congress (WJC) Swiss representative Dr. Gerhart Riegner. Riegner tried to contact WJC President Rabbi Stephen Wise through secure channels, only to have his message intercepted by the US State Department. When Wise later heard the news from the British, the State Department confirmed it, but asked Wise not to publicize the information until it was reconfirmed that fall. Even then, America's doors were not opened to Jews fleeing Hitler. Subsequently, the State Department sent a cable to US consulates in neutral countries to close the secret communication channel, signaling a disinterest by the State Department in the Jews' fate.

Meanwhile, Polish secret courier Jan Karski toured the US from 1943-45 in a desperate effort to publicize what he had learned about the massive murder of European Jews. Meeting with Roosevelt, Rabbi Wise, and prominent journalists, he also published a book about the Warsaw Ghetto which became a Book-of-the-Month Club selection. By 1943 word was out about Hitler's plan to exterminate all European Jews—yet Congressional resolutions which would have provided refuge to the prospective victims never even made it to a vote.

Thanks, however, to diligent research by Treasury Department lawyer Josiah DuBois, which exposed the State Department's cover-up of the Final Solution, on January 13, 1944, US Treasury Department officials sent Secretary of the Treasury Henry Morganthau a memo called "The Acquiescence of This Government in the Murder of the Jews." Finally, Roosevelt set up a War Refugee Board, which had to be privately-funded, but which eventually succeeded in saving about 200,000 Jews.

Physical Violence Against Jews

Compared to people of color in this country, Jews have experienced little physical violence—and none of it has been state-sponsored. Foremost was the Georgia lynching of Jewish factory owner Leo Frank in 1913, who was also President of the local B'nai B'rith chapter. Set up by false testimony, he was convicted of murdering 13-year-old worker Mary Phagan; after his death sentence was commuted to life imprisonment, the enraged community kidnapped him from the prison farm and murdered him. 3,000 Jews fled Georgia soon afterwards.

Washington Post reporter Kathy Sawyer recently uncovered that the Frank lynching was committed by some of Marietta, Georgia's most prestigious townspeople, as revealed in deathbed confessions to their families. By all accounts the lynching was well-planned and coldly calculated—and it led to the re-invigoration of the Ku Klux Klan, while simultaneously helping build B'nai B'rith's Anti-Defamation League.

Meanwhile, as Jews were being rounded up and gassed in Eastern Europe, gangs from Father Coughlin's right-wing anti-Communist United Christian Front attacked Jewish adults and children on the streets of Boston and New York, desecrating synagogues and Jewish cemeteries, and vandalizing Jewish-owned businesses.

And although the War Refugee Board, backed by numerous Jewish organizations, frantically urged the federal government to bomb railway lines to Auschwitz, no action was taken. Michael Berenbaum insists that by May 1944 the US government knew what was happening in Auschwitz, and that the Air Force had the capability for such a mission, at one point dropping over 1,000 bombs on a factory nearby. Instead, they focused on defeating the Nazis—a defeat which came too late to save millions of lives. Arguably, the decision to do nothing else to save the victims' lives can be seen as culpability akin to violence.

In the post-war period, the US executed young Jewish Communists Julius and Ethel Rosenberg, who were victims of Cold War anti-Communist hysteria, combined with anti-Semitism. Accused of conspiring to sell classified atomic secrets to the Russians, the evidence against them was inconclusive. Meanwhile, Jewish temples were bombed in the South in 1957-58; and in 1964, two young (white) Jewish civil rights workers, Michael Schwerner and Andrew Goodman, were murdered along with their African-American colleague James Chaney.

As recently as the summer of 1999, three synagogues were firebombed in Sacramento, CA; Orthodox Jews were viciously assaulted in Chicago; and Jewish schoolchildren were critically shot in an attack on a Los Angles Jewish day school. Significantly, each of these crimes was also connected to fatal attacks on gay men or people of color.

Anti-Semitism On The Left

As Michael Lerner reminds us, anti-Semitism is most to be feared from the conservative Christian Right, not from the Left—and the Left has been a key voice in acknowledging anti-Semitism as an ongoing oppression with a commitment to eliminating it. That said, many leading progressive Jewish activists from Lerner to Irena Klepfisz (whose father died helping lead the Warsaw Ghetto uprising) admonish the Left, non-Jews and Jews alike, for buying into the assumption that Jews, as Jews, are bidding for vast control in the world, and are some of those most responsible for world problems.

A major critique accuses the Left, including the Women's Movement, of consistently discounting Jewish oppression and branding those who raise the issue self-indulgent or competing for "victim status." Those who call attention to anti-Semitism can be accused of diverting energy from more important struggles—implying that there is not enough room on a progressive agenda for Jewish oppression. [Note: This is a complex issue, since white Jewish leftists sometimes do unawarely subvert anti-racist agendas to instead focus on Jewish oppression, thus showing their white privilege. This Jewish racism is often the result, however, of the anti-Semitism of ignoring and/or diminishing the importance of Jewish pain—which does not excuse the racism of the agenda-diversion.] Part of the discounting includes the Left not taking seriously those who speak from a place of heartfelt connection to their Jewishness.

Leftist anti-Semitism can also show itself as singling out Israel for its horrific human rights abuses, without acknowledging that Israel is not the only state committing atrocities. Need we remind ourselves of Columbia, Burma, Zaire, Afghanistan, including the US treatment of Iraqi people? Related to this is the way that Jews are either expected to be "better," or are seen as worse, than others—but not as human beings like everyone else, with many strengths, and a few gnarly spots as well. And human rights activist Susan Freundlich points out that "Where anti-Semitism really shows itself is in the spilling over of the rightful condemnation of Israeli government policies into the hatred of Jewish people as a whole—where the criticism of a policy becomes the blanket condemnation of a people."

Jewish Voice for Peace co-Director Liat Weingart recently wrote about the lack of understanding of Jewish oppression in the progressive movement—including "the enormous cost that we have paid to make ourselves invisible in the larger society, and on the left, for fear of being scapegoated for the corrupt policies of either the US or Israel." She referred to non-Jewish leftist colleagues who blame Jews for "the horrific policies of the government …of Israel, though we are fighting those policies," as well as blaming Jews "for controlling the media, for initiating a war with Iraq." When she pointed out that these statements have "undercurrents of anti-Semitism," she has been met with denial. Calling for the issue of anti-Semitism to be part of the agenda of a progressive movement, along with other oppressions, she explained that "anti-Semitism is different than other forms of oppression. The existence of Jews in positions of power in this country does not mean that anti-Semitism does not exist."

When Jewish oppression is discounted, Jews absorb the message to be silent and to ignore the invisibility and vulnerability Jews may feel as Jews. It's useful to remember here, as communities working together for a social justice agenda, the words of Chicana activist and writer Cherie Moraga, who reminded a multicultural group of Jews and non-Jews to each take responsibility for their own ignorance, and to "refuse to give up on each other."

Conclusion: Resisting Victimization

The good news is that, despite the accelerated brutal repression of the Israeli government towards Palestinians (which I suggest is a function of unhealed Jewish fear, as a response to centuries of persecution—a fear manipulated by despots—but that is the subject of another article!), which has brought more anti-Semitism to the surface, US Jews are not victims any longer.

In this country, most Jews have gained economic stability, civil rights, and political power. In 1958 anti-Semitism was finally eliminated from all prayers by Pope John XXIII; and in 1965, the Second Vatican Council officially exonerated Jews for the death of Christ, repudiating the idea that Jews were rejected by God for not accepting Jesus as savior. And just as the Holocaust has become the historical experience which unites American Jews, it is also true that anti-Semitism is not integrated into a broadly-accepted political philosophy in this country.

Yet of course it is more complicated than that. US Jews must still contend with what Melanie Kaye/Kantrowitz calls "Christianism"—a system that honors and rewards everything Christian, thus marginalizing, and sometimes targeting, everything non-Christian. But Jews can also ally with other non-Christians to combat this oppression.

And as Kaye/Kantrowitz also reminds us, while Jewish oppression has been somewhat mitigated since World War II by the development of some institutionalized Jewish power, often it is this very success for which Jews are blamed. While anti-Semitism works to single out Jews and make Jews visible, anti-Semitism itself remains invisible to most non-Jews—which serves to make Jews feel only more exposed.

Hurtful stereotypes, insidious scapegoating, the disregard of anti-Semitism, and occasional violence continue, battering Jewish self-esteem and heightening Jewish feelings of vulnerability—even though externally Jews appear successful and secure, and in fact are standing on much more solid ground than ever before. Because it's also true that Jews are here, Jews have survived, and many Jews are thriving.

As Jews who care about Jews here, and about Jews in Israel, we need to confront all the complexities: the reality of past Jewish oppression and how Jews still carry fear from that experience—especially the Holocaust; the current increase in anti-Semitic incidents in Europe; the reality of relative Jewish security here in the United States, despite a recent rise in anti-Semitism; and the reality of Israeli government policies against Palestinians—that are only bringing more Israeli deaths, and less security for Israel.

Just as anti-Semitism has been rising, anti-Arab racism inside Israel is rising as well, just as racism in this country has exploded against Muslims and people of Arab descent since 9/11. As Jews with a proud heritage of social justice, we cannot let ourselves take comfort in the badge of victimization: when we target anti-Semitism, we must also target racism in this country and in Israel.

And as Jews, let's notice how our fear can paralyze us; let's acknowledge that old place inside us that starts to feel "everyone hates the Jews." It's not our fault if we feel this way—but this time let's work through these feelings, so that we don't take out our fear or grief or outrage against any other people, be they Palestinian, or Muslim, or African-American—or Jewish. We deserve compassion and understanding, just as we need to offer that to others.

Let's stand against the oppression of Jews and the oppression of Palestinians—against the oppression of all people who are marginalized because of their skin color or ethnicity or social class or body size or gender or sexual orientation or age or disability. Let's value all lives as precious and worth protecting, and not allow any people to be demeaned or vilified. Let's do all we can to build a movement for peace and justice for all peoples, not a movement of hatred towards any people. Let's build alliances and bridges between us, not walls and buffer zones.

[Sources: "The Rising Cost of Whiteness" by Melanie Kaye/Kantrowitz, Anti-Semitism in America by Leonard Dinnerstein, Fighting to Become Americans by Riv-Ellen Prell, The Ethnic Myth by Stephen Steinberg, "Pluralism and its Discontents" by Cheryl Greenberg, Jewish Power by J.J. Goldberg, Uprooting Racism and Who Decides? Who Benefits? Who Pays? A Guide to the US Ruling Class Power Elite (working title, in publication) by Paul Kivel, "The People In-between" by Rabbi Robert J. Marx; "The People In-between" Gender and Assimilation in Modern Jewish History by Paula Hyman, Jewish Self-Hatred by Sander Gilman, The World Must Know by Michael Berenbaum, The Socialism of Fools by Michael Lerner, Dreams of an Insomniac by Irena Klepfisz, "Hard Ground: Jewish Identity, Racism, and Anti-Semitism" by Elly Bulkin (Cherie Moraga quote)], A Different Mirror by Ronald Takaki, How the Jews Became White Folks & What That Says About Race in America by Karen Brodkin, Diversity in the Power Elite by Richard Zweigenhaft & G. William Domhoff, the 2001-2003 United Jewish Communities "National Jewish Population Study," personal communication with Susan Freundlich, and email communication with Riv-Ellen Prell, Liat Weingart, and Mitchell Plitnick.]

Penny Rosenwasser is completing her doctoral dissertation on the psychological effects of anti-Semitism on Jews. She published *Voices From a 'Promised Land': Palestinian and Israeli Peace Activists Speak Their Hearts*, (Curbstone Press, 1992). She belongs to Kehilla Synagogue and is a member of the Coordinating Committee of Jewish Voice for Peace.

ARTICLE 8

IS CRITICIZING ISRAEL ANTI-SEMITIC?
Chuck Sher

This paper is a response to the claim that the Petaluma Progressives' weekly downtown protests "express hatred against the state of Israel," as counter-demonstrators claim. As the founder of the Progressives, I would respectfully disagree with this assessment. Here's why:

As a Jew, I understand the fear that our people have for the safety of fellow Jews, and I know the distrust that this fear can create. There are certainly centuries of persecution to back up these feelings. But approaching the world out of fear can become a self-fulfilling prophecy. Instead of creating security, it can create over-reaction, callousness towards the suffering of others, and a justification of the use of excessive force–which then turns into an endless cycle of violence and revenge. This is what is happening in Palestine and Israel, especially in the last three years of Ariel Sharon's exclusive use of force as the sole approach to a very complex set of problems.

Palestinian suicide bombings are also an utterly reprehensible tactic and hundreds of innocent Israelis have been needlessly killed in the current fighting. It is even possible that there would already be a just peace in place if the Palestinians had been able to mount a sustained nonviolent response to the Israeli Occupation. The fact that they didn't is a real tragedy for both peoples. So why don't we put equal blame on the Palestinians for the ongoing violence? There are several good reasons for this.

1) Israel's violence is of a different order.
   Israel's army is the fourth largest in the world, with state-of-the-art military equipment supplied by billions of our tax dollars every year. For the last year the IDF has systematically terrorized the Palestinian population, injuring over 20,000 Palestinians, keeping millions locked in their houses with little respite for months at a time, destroying their economy which has led to widespread malnutrition, destroying every vestige of Palestinian civil society, cultural centers, government offices having nothing to do with resistance to the occupation, day care centers, etc. Palestinian suicide missions are a sign of Palestinian weakness, not strength—a last-ditch measure of desperation carried out by people who can no longer tolerate their homes, families and friends being blown up around them.

2) Israel initiated the current level of lethal force.
   There was sporadic Palestinian violence during the Oslo years, but nothing like the magnitude we've seen in the last three years, and even that was in response to Israeli violence, like Baruch Goldstein's massacre of 29 Muslim worshippers in a mosque in Hebron in 1994. Far from orchestrating this violence, Arafat's PA during the Oslo years was arresting and torturing Hamas militants on Israel's behalf, an activity that became politically, and even physically, impossible once Israeli forces re-occu-

pied most of the West Bank in the current fighting.

The current intifada started with Ariel Sharon's provocative visit to the Al-Aksa mosque with 1000 Israeli armed guards in tow. The following day there was a predictable Palestinian demonstration in Jerusalem, which the Israeli police could have dispersed using non-lethal means, but they didn't. They open-fired on the crowd, leaving at least 6 Palestinians dead and hundreds injured. During the next month, 125 Palestinians were killed, mostly unarmed demonstrators throwing rocks at well-defended Israeli soldiers—-on Palestinian territory, by the way, not in Israel itself. Only after this had gone on for a month did the first suicide bombing in the current intifada occur. This is a crucial fact that belies the claim that Israeli actions are "in response" to suicide bombings. As Human Rights Watch reported at the time, "Israeli security forces have committed by far the most serious and systematic violations. We documented excessive and indiscriminate use of lethal force, arbitrary killings and collective punishment…that far exceed any possible military necessity."

3) Correcting US media bias.
One sign at our vigils states: "Innocent Palestinians are being shot every day." This is merely a statement of fact. Eighty Palestinians were killed in the first week of March alone. And over 2000 Palestinians have been killed in the past three and a half years—the majority of them unarmed people killed by IDF troops who have opened fire at demonstrations, at firefighters trying to put out

fires, at medical personnel trying to evacuate the wounded, at journalists, UN relief workers, an elderly person on a donkey who wandered into a "closed military area," people killed when their homes were demolished around them, people killed by Israeli snipers for the crime of venturing outdoors during extended "curfew" periods, people killed by bombs dropped on crowded apartment buildings, kids killed by Israeli tanks while throwing rocks, and on and on. (As for the claim that only terrorists are being targeted, for one it is patently untrue; and for two the Israeli government has no legal or moral right to be judge, jury, and executioner of "suspected militants" who are assassinated without due process, without the right of defense, etc. This policy of Sharon's is completely illegal under international law.)

Our corporate media has prominent headlines, photos and TV footage whenever there are Israeli victims of random violence, but severely downplays, or totally ignores, the much more frequent and systematic violence perpetrated by the Israeli government. Our sign is an attempt to rectify this imbalance.

4) The illegal Israeli occupation of Palestinian land is, in itself, a series of acts of violence. Just as armed robbery is an act of violence, even if no one is hurt, the Israeli occupation of the West Bank and Gaza has been one long series of forcible expropriations of Palestinian land. This was made possible by the unconditional diplomatic support of the US government since 1972, which has

allowed Israel to ignore the overwhelming consensus of world opinion that their occupation of Palestinian land is illegal under international law. At this point, well over 50% of the Occupied Territories consist of illegal Jewish-only settlements, Jewish-only bypass roads, and closed Israeli military areas.

5) Israel's illegal occupation is the root cause of the violence, and so their refusal to dismantle that occupation means they have the lion's share of the responsibility for the continuation of the violence. As Israel's former Attorney General, Michael Ben-Yair wrote in Ha'aretz (3/3/02), "We enthusiastically chose to become a colonial society, ignoring international treaties, expropriating lands, transferring settlers from Israel to the occupied territories, engaging in theft and finding justification for all these activities… In effect, we established an apartheid regime in the occupied territories immediately following their capture. That oppressive regime exists to this day."

Israel might be faulted for over-zealousness but not ultimate responsibility for the conflict if the Palestinians were an implacable enemy, unwilling to negotiate a reasonable peace agreement. But this myth, while perhaps comforting to some, is simply historically inaccurate. Since 1988 when the Palestinian Authority officially accepted Israel's right to exist in peace and security within their pre-1967 borders, there have been numerous chances to trade land for peace, all of which Israel rejected out-of-hand. Most recently, the entire Arab League, including the Palestinian Authority, unanimously voted in March of 2002 to endorse the Saudi "Land For Peace" proposal, which would have given Israel a permanent peace, including full normalization of relations with all its Arab neighbors, including the Palestinians. Sharon's response to this historic offer was to invade Jenin, Nablus, and the rest of the West Bank, during which time severe breaches of the Geneva Conventions were committed, amounting to war crimes, according to Human Rights Watch, Amnesty International, and B'tselem.

Until Israel gives back all the land that is not theirs, the conflict will never end. So the ultimate responsibility does lie with Israel to bring a just solution to the table (Barak's "generous offer" at Camp David was woefully short of a just solution. See "From Jew To Jew: Why We Should Oppose the Israeli Occupation of the West Bank and Gaza" for an in-depth discussion of this question. It is available online at www.jewishvoiceforpeace.org or by writing Jewish Voice For Peace, 1611 Telegraph Avenue, Suite 500, Oakland, CA 94612. First justice, then peace. It cannot happen the other way around, as you can see if you put yourself in Palestinian shoes for just a minute. And this is why our vigil signs "blame" Israel. They, and they alone, hold the key to a just and peaceful solution.

Conclusion

Instead of blaming the messenger, I would request that concerned people work to change the reality. Just as it is not anti-American to oppose Bush's indefensible military adventures, neither is it anti-Israel to oppose the policies of state terrorism practiced by Sharon's government.

In my opinion, Ariel Sharon's actions in the past three years are well on the way to ruining the high moral standing of our people, developed over thousands of years. And he also bears the lion's share of responsibility for the upswing in anti-Semitic incidents worldwide, as people become enraged at Israel's tactics. Sticking your head in the sand and pretending that the world will not notice what Sharon is doing, is just not a realistic option. By trying to change Israel's policies, I believe we are in fact fighting the root cause of increased anti-Semitism.

So are our protests "expressions of hatred of Israel"? I don't believe so. "Hate the sin, but not the sinner" is closer to our feelings. Indeed, I believe that our efforts to bring US and Jewish public opinion to bear against the illegal Israeli occupation of the West Bank and Gaza offers the only real path to peace and security for Israelis. Anything else is just a prescription for endless bloodshed. As Jimmy Carter wrote in the Washington Post, "It is unlikely that real progress can be made…as long as Israel insists on its settlement policy, illegal under international laws." The day that the international community convinces Israel to live up to its obligations under the Geneva Conventions, and remove their illegal settlements and illegal military occupation from Palestinian territory, is the day that peace will become possible.

Chuck Sher is a musician, businessperson, and long-time political and environmental activist in Petaluma, CA. He is the founder of The Petaluma Progressives and the author of JVP's most widely distributed pamphlet: *From Jew to Jew: Why We Should Oppose the Occupation of the West Bank and Gaza.*

Jewish Voice for Peace

קול יהודי לשלום

**Israelis and Palestinians.
Two Peoples, One Future.**

Are you a Jewish voice for peace? Are you an ally?

Do you want to build a voice for the silent majority of American Jews and allies who want an end to the occupation and settlements, and to the needless deaths of Palestinians and Israelis?

The power of that voice depends on you.

Through grassroots organizing, education, advocacy, and media outreach, Jewish Voice for Peace works to achieve a lasting peace that recognizes the aspirations of both Israelis and Palestinians for security and self–determination.

Become a member of Jewish Voice for Peace to promote a US foreign policy based on peace, democracy, human rights, and respect for international law.

Become A Member

Go to our website at www.jewishvoiceforpeace.org, click on "join us." and have your credit card ready. Or tear off this membership form and send it to the address below.

- $50 Regular Member
- $18 Student/Low Income Member
- $36 Supporting Member
- $500 Peacemakers Circle Member
- $250 Sustaining Membe
- $100 Contributing Member

Name_____

Organization_____

Address_____

City/State/Zip_____

Country_____

Phone_____ Email_____

Amount Enclosed_____ Please return membership form and dues to:

Jewish Voice for Peace • 1611 Telegraph Avenue, Suite 500 • Oakland, CA 94612 • USA
510 465 1777 • info@jewishvoiceforpeace.org

www.JewishVoiceforPeace.org